Marriages
of
Sussex County
Virginia
- 1754-1810 -

Compiled By:
Catherine Lindsay Knorr

Southern Historical Press, Inc.
Greenville, South Carolina

SOUTHERN HISTORICAL PRESS, INC.
PO BOX 1267
Greenville, SC   29601

ISBN #0-89308-257-0

Printed in the United States of America

TO

MRS. LEWIS LINWOOD CHAPMAN

(BLANCHE ADAMS)

FROM WHOM I LEARNED.

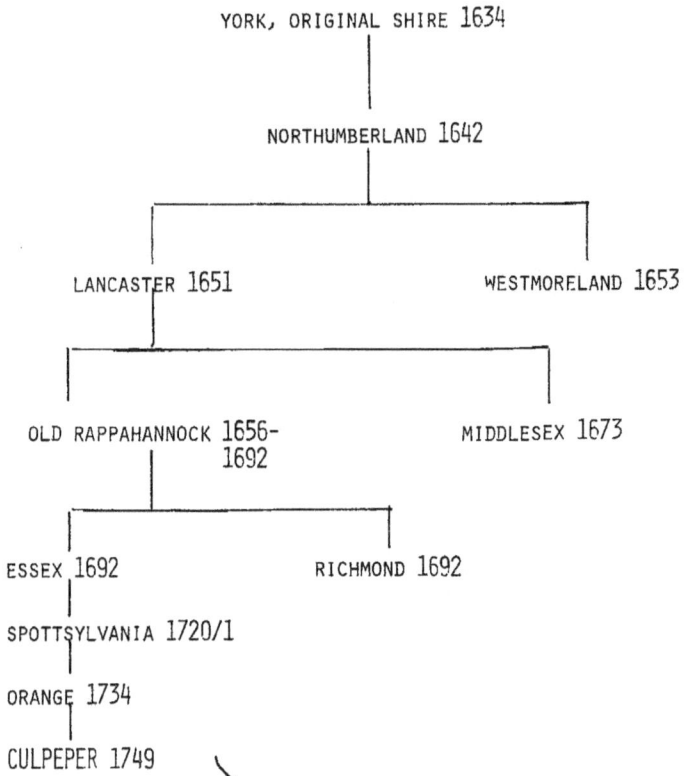

YORK, ORIGINAL SHIRE 1634

NORTHUMBERLAND 1642

LANCASTER 1651

WESTMORELAND 1653

OLD RAPPAHANNOCK 1656-1692

MIDDLESEX 1673

ESSEX 1692

RICHMOND 1692

SPOTTSYLVANIA 1720/1

ORANGE 1734

CULPEPER 1749

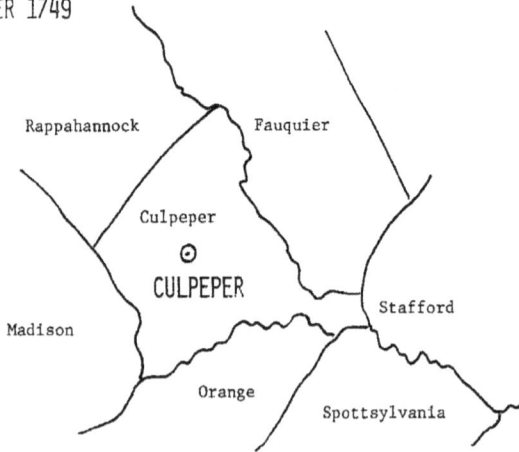

Rappahannock

Fauquier

Culpeper

⊙
CULPEPER

Stafford

Madison

Orange

Spottsylvania

PREFACE

Virginia named fourteen of her counties for her Governors of which Culpeper is one: named for Thomas, Lord Culpeper who served from 1680 to 1683 as governor of VIrginia. He was the grandfather of Thomas, Lord Fairax, his only child, Catherine, having married Thomas, 5th Baron Fairfax of Cameron. It was to take up the vast estate in Virginia, inherited from his grandfather that motivated Thomas, 6th Baron Fairfax to come to Virginia. (Complete Peerage 2nd Ed., Vol III p 364, note A and 365: Long's Virginia County Names pp 136-137.)

Culpeper County lies in one of the lovliest parts of Virginia, just south of Fauquier, both homes of famous hunt clubs. The terrain is rolling, beautiful for the eye to see and restful to the spirit.

18 May 1749 is the birthday of Culpeper County. When an "Act for dividing the County of Orange" was passed by the General Assembly 23 March 1748 Culpeper became the northern half. (Hening's Statutes at Large, Vol. V p 408.) The Rappahamock River divides the two.

The first minute book has been lost but the deed books show that the first County Court was held on the above date, no place mentioned. On Thursday 15 June 1749 Court was held at the residence of Robert Coleman. Roger Dixon was Clerk from 1749 until 1772; James Jameson from 1772 until 1810 and the third Clerk, William Broaddus served from 1810 until his death in 1841.

The Culpeper Deed Books are extant from 1749. Deed Book A 1749-1753 records on page 1 an indenture dated 15 April 1749. David Kinkead and Winifred, his wife of the Parish of St. Anne's in the County of Albemarle to William Duncan of the Parish of St. Mark's in the County of Orange; 660 acres in Parish of St. Mark's in the County of Orange for 5 shillings sterling money. Witnesses: Samuel Scott, John Roberts, Jr., Rawley Duncan and William Duncan, Jr. Culpeper Court held for the said county at the home of Robert Coleman on Thursday 15 June 1749 this indenture was proved by the oaths of Samuel Scott, John Roberts, Jr., Rawley Duncan and William Duncan, Jr. Rogert Dixon, Clerk of the Court.

In the first extant Minute Book 1763-1764, the first surviving page is 271, the date 17 March 1763. It lists the Captains of Militia appointed that day: William Brown, John Brown, James Rucker, Ephraim Rucker and John Slaughter, all of whom produced their commissions from His Honor, the Governor, Francis Fauquier. Under William Green, Esq., their County Lieutenant they took the oath to His Majesty George III, his person and government. Minutes of these court proceedings are signed by Ambrose Powell. Gentlemen Justices present were: Robert Green, Benjamin Roberts, Henry Field, Jr., William Williams and James Slaughter.

St. Mark's Parish was formed 1 January 1731, at which time it was in Orange but fell in Culpeper when that county was established 1748/9. Twelve vestrymen were elected: Goodrich Lightfoot, Henry Field, Francis Kirtly, James Barbour, Robert Slaughter, John Finlason, Francis Slaughter, Thomas Staunton, Benjamin Cave, Robert Green, and Samuel Ball. Robert Slaughter and Francis Slaughter were first church wardens and William Peyton the first clerk. They had no rector but the visiting clergy, Rev. Mr. De Butts and Rev. Mr. Purit. Church wardens bought record books and parish lines were surveyed. Zachary Lewis was their attorney and Robert Turner collector of tithes. First elected Rector of St. Mark's was the Rev. Mr. John Beckett in 1733. (Slaughter's St. Mark's Parish, Culpeper County, 1877).

The Rev. Mr. John Thompson became rector 10 June 1740; the Rev. Mr. Edward Jones 1772; the Rev. Mr. James Stevenson in 1780;, then the Rev. Mr. John Woodville. In 1877 when Dr. Slaughter wrote his history the Parish register, as he said, "lies before me". What a loss that it cannot now be found! Lack of space forbids that the early vestrymen be named but here are some of the families: Lightfoot, Staunton, Roberts, Triplett, Field, Kirtly, Clayton, Catlett, Brown, Dillard, Slaughter, Powell, Pendleton, Ball, Barbour, Cave, Green, Peyton, Pollard, Gaines, Yancy and many others.

Pre-revolution physicians in Culpeper were: Dr. Andrew Craig, Dr. Thomas Howison, Dr. James Biggs and Dr. Michael Wallace. Lawyers for the same period were: Zachary Lewis, John Mercer, John Lewis and Gabriel Jones.

At the beginning of the Revolution, Culpeper, Orange and Fauquier organized a regiment of "Minute Men". (Howes "Virginia" pp 237-238). The Culpeper Corps dressed in forest green hunting shirts, each man wearing a leather belt around his shoulders with a tomahawk and scalping knife! Their flag was equally as agressive as their appearance. It had depicted on it a rattle snake with twelve rattles, the head for Virginia and a rattle for each of the other colonies. On the flag, above the coiled snake were words "The Culpeper Minute Men" and below "Liberty or Death" amd "Don't Tread On Me". (Long's Virginia County Names p 141).

To this good day that famous emblem graces the top of a folder published and distributed by the Culpeper Chamber of Commerce.

Prosaic as this type of book is, a great deal of delving into the history, background, inheritance and habits of the people is required to present it intelligently. Culpeper is fascinating. It was from Culpeper that the famous "Knights of the Golden Horseshoe" started their trek west and drank the King's health on top of the highest Blue Ridge peak. Governor Alexander Spottswood, their leader, lived in Culpeper.

In 1785 came a separation of Church and State and at last the Episcopal Church was free to elect Bishops and frame a constitution of its own. Before the Revolution the ministers were compelled by law to keep a record of the list of baptisms and marriages but after the Revolution the only legal requirement was that every marriage had to be reported to the Clerk of the County Court. These we call Ministers' Returns. Since the Culpeper marriage bonds do not exist the ministers' returns are all we have. Then in 1802 a blow fell. All the parish registers were seized as the property of the State and many were lost in court houses after they ceased to be cherished by the current rector of the parish.

It was about this time that the ministers of the Baptist faith planted churches in Culpeper and proclaimed their doctrines. (Semple's History of the Rise and Progress of the Baptists in Virginia, Beale's revised edition 1894).

Of the 38 ministers making returns to the Culpeper Court for the period that this book covers, 1781-1815, twenty-one are unidentified as to denomination, one a Methodist, one an Episcopalian, one a Lutheran and fourteen are Baptists. It does not always follow that the principals of a wedding were of the same church as the minister who married them.

One thing emerges: the ministers were even more casual spellers than the clerks. We find Roda for Rhoda, Aron for Aaron, Elener for Eleanor, Stevin for Stephen, even Sharlotte for Charlotte. But how grateful we are to them for setting it all down and how freely we forgive them their spelling!

Every source of information has been carefully checked and all versions conscientiously given. Even the wills were checked for possible parentage of the contracting parties. Many times a marriage appears twice with different dates. The minister, being human, forgot he had filed it once and sent it in again. The first date is apt to be correct but both are given, so you be the judge.

There are some acknowledgements I must make and it is a pleasure to give credit to those who make sucn an effort ot help me make my Culpeper marriages accurate: Mr. A. Roberts Pulliam who located for me the fragment of St. Mark's Parish Register that has survived; Miss Mary Lee Somerville who copied it for me and last but by no means least Mrs. H. Franklin Bywaters, Deputy Clerk. who cheerfully checked page after page of discrepancies for me. I could not have gone to press with out Nelly May and her tireless efforts to have every thing just right. So my debt to the helpful, courteous Culpeper Countians grows and grows.

Mrs. H. A. Knorr

27 August 1805. John ABBOTT and Elizabeth Heaton. Minister, Reuben Finnell. p 13

6 July 1785. John ABLE and Frances Fennel. Minister, William Mason, Baptist. p 1

17 April 1794. John ADAMS and Margaret Calvert. Minister, John Pickett, Baptist. Margaret Calvert b 1770, dau. George and Lydia Beck Ralls, who m. 7 February 1764. p 1

13 October 1796. Thomas ADAMS and Anne Houton. Minister, Charles Yates. p 1

20 February 1797. Thomas ADAMS and Anne Houton. Minister, Charles Yates. Both dates given. p 1

10 September 1784. Ambrose ADKINS and Frankey Mansfield. Minister, William Mason, Baptist. Green's notes on Culpeper say Frances Marrifield. p 1

26 May 1795. James AINES and Winny McQueen. Minister, Lewis Corbin. Green's notes on Culpeper say McGuinn. p 1

27 August 1782. William ALEXANDER and Frankey Rucker. Minister, George Eve, Baptist. p 1

6 June 1815. Benjamin ALLEN and Elizabeth Paul. Minister, William Mason, Baptist. p 2

21 April 1814. Curchill ALLEN and Polly Walden. Minister, Lewis Conner, Baptist. p 2

22 December 1788. James ALLEN and Sarah Chapman. Minister, William Mason, Baptist. p 1

8 February 1792. James ALLEN and Mary Hunt. Minister, James Garnett, Baptist. p 1

19 September 1799. James ALLEN and Betty Chilton. Minister, Frederick Kabler. p 1

25 September 1806. James ALLEN and Eliza C. White. Minister, Lewis Conner, Baptist. p 18

24 April 1812. Newman ALLEN and Peggy White. Minister, Lewis Conner, Baptist. p 2

13 January 1799. Wesley ALLEN and Susanna Gaines. Minister, Charles Yates. p 1

7 April 1814. John ALMOND and Jane Bengham. Minister, William Mason, Baptist. p 2

22 February 1786. Philip AMISS and Ann Tapp. Minister, John Pickett, Baptist. p 1

4 September 1786. Philip AMISS and Ann Tapp. Minister, John Pickett, Baptist. Same as above - both dates given. p 1

2 March 1786. Augustine ANDERSON and Nancy Underwood. Minister, George Eve, Baptist. Green's Notes on Culpeper say Annie Underwood. p 1

- - 1804. Elijah ANDERSON and Mary Priest. Minister, Lewis Conner, Baptist. p 17

3 November 1789. George ANDERSON and Bersheby Clark. Minister, George Eve, Baptist. Green's Notes on Culpeper say Berkley Clark. p 1

9 March 1786. John ANDERSON and Lucy Sutton. Minister, Isham Tatum. p 1

18 December 1800. John ANDERSON and Nancy Little. Minister, Absalom Little. p 2

16 December 1792. Josiah ANDERSON and Elizabeth Richerson. Minister, John Swindler. p 1

9 October 1799. Aaron ANTRAM and Charlotte King. Minister, Frederick Kabler. p 1

13 November 1799. Thomas ANTRAM and Esther Sharpe. Minister, James Barnett, Baptist. p 1

1 January 1793. John APPLEBY and Mary Long. Minister, William Mason, Baptist. p 1

30 - 1788. Edmund ARCHER and Susanna Piner. Minister, Isham Tatum. Green's Notes on Culpeper say Pener. p 1

30 October 1808. Thomson ASHBY and Ann S. Menefee. Minister William Mason, Baptist. p 16

12 November 1805. William ASHBY and Lucy Strother. Minister, Lewis Conner, Baptist. p 18

31 May 1800. John ASHER and Betsy Burbridge. Minister, Frederick Kabler. p 1

26 December 1805. Waller R. ASHER and Eliza Shannon. Minister, Lewis Conner, Baptist. p 18

16 March 1797. William ASHER and Elizabeth Sharpe. Minister, Frederick
Kabler. p 1

2 September 1802. Benjamin ASKIN and Lucy Settle. Minister, Reuben
Finnell. p 11

31 January 1795. William ASKINS and Catherine Jones. Minister, Lewis
Corbin. p 1

24 August 1785. John ATHE and Dorcas Cullen. Minister, John Price,
Baptist. Tax list says Athie. p 1

8 November 1792. Cornelius AUSTIN and Eleanor Butler. Minister, William
Mason, Baptist. p 1

20 February 1810. Lewis AYLOR and Nancy Creal. Minister, Lewis Conner,
Baptist. p 2

24 March 1795. Michael AYLOR and Sarah Boughorn. Minister, William
Carpenter, Lutheran. p 1

1 October 1802. John BAILY and Alice Paton. Minister, Frederick Kabler.
p 8

29 March 1791. James BAINES and Frances Thompson. Minister, George Eve,
Baptist. p 7

23 March 1799. Jacob BAKER and Lydia Trimble. Minister, Frederick
Kabler. p 7

12 March 1799. John BALCHELDER and Sally Pup. Minister, Reuben Finnell.
p 7

15 August 1803. Joseph BALDEN and Betsey Dillard. Minister, Charles
Yates. p 9

17 January 1799. Ezra BALL and Ann Dillin. Minister, Reuben Finnell. p 7

4 October 1815. Peter BALDEN and Amy Smith. Minister, Lewis Conner,
Baptist. p 23

21 December 1792. John BALL and Polly Ester Gibbs. Minister, Isham
Tatum. p 6

22 October 1807. Samuel BALL and Ann Thud. Minister, Lewis Conner,
Baptist. p 19

3 June 1796. Willis BALLANCE and Joicy Green. Minister, Lewis Corbin.
Green's Notes on Culpeper say Joyce. p 6

23 April 1781. Curtis BALLARD and Esther Gaines. Minister, Elijah Craig, Baptist. p 4

22 December 1791. Johnson BALLARD and Betty Eastham. Minister, George Eve, Baptist. p 5

19 January 1786. Larkin BALLARD and Elizabeth Gaines. Minister, George Eve, Baptist. p 3

11 May 1791. John BALLERN and Anne Cook. Minister, William Carpenter, Lutheran. p 6

16 January 1806. William BALLINGER and Elizabeth Hughes. Minister, Lewis Conner, Baptist. p 18

4 May 1794. Michael BANNEN and Frances Brown. Married, at St. Mark's Gleve by the Rev. John Woodville, Rector of St. Mark's Parish. Episcopal Church. St. Mark's Parish Register.

23 January 1808. William BARBEE and Fanny Curtis. Minister, Reuben Finnell. p 15

24 March 1796. William BARBOUR and Elizabeth White. Minister, William Mason, Baptist. p 5

16 June 1789. George BARGER and Hannah Boon. Minister, William Mason, Baptist. Tax list says Bargo. p 5

3 August 1793. John BARGER and Anne Swindler. Minister, John Swindler. p 3

24 May 1789. Joshua BARLER and Rhoda Thomas. Minister, William Mason, Baptist. Barlow? Baylor? p 5

27 January 1789. Ephraim BARLOW and Mary Ann Carter. Minister, William Carpenter, Lutheran. p 3

19 April 1794. Benjamin BARNES and Eleanor Stapleman. Minister, John Swindler. p 6

31 December 1792. James BARNES and Polly Hill. Minister, William Mason, Baptist. p 6

25 January 1787. Martin BARNES and Rhoda Sampson. Minister, William Mason, Baptist. p 4

18 May 1786. Shadrack BARNES and Frances Mozingo. Minister, John Pickett, Baptist. p 4

25 October 1790. William BARNES and Elizabeth Marshall. Minister, William Mason, Baptist. p 6

25 July 1797. Zachariah BARNES and Ginnet Roberts. Minister, Frederick Kabler. p 6

19 December 1795. Daniel BARNETT and Ruthy McGruder. Minister, John Pickett, Baptist. Green's Notes on Culpeper say Magruder. p 7

- - -. Lawrence BARNETT and Catherine Vass or Voss. Green's Notes on Culpeper p 57

10 December 1794. Richard BARNETT and Sarah Utterback. Minister, John Hickerson, Baptist. p 7

4 November 1797. William BARNETT and Sarah Matthews. Minister, John Pickett, Baptist. p 7

14 April 1791. William BARRAN and Lucy Twentiman. Minister, James Garnett, Baptist. p 3

21 June 1808. Edmund BASYE and Caty Thomas. Minister, Lewis Conner, Baptist. p 20

- - 1786. Henry BASYE and Elizabeth James. Green's Notes on Culpeper. p 57

11 December 1793. John BASYE and Catherine Basye. Minister, John Pickett, Baptist. p 3

28 November 1781. William BATES, Jr., and Elizabeth Harris. Minister, George Eve, Baptist. p 4

3 December 1781. William BATES, Sr., and Mary Harris. Minister, George Eve, Baptist. p 4

5 February 1812. Moses BAUGHAM and Sarah Yowell. Minister, Lewis Conner, Baptist. p 22

6 March 1797. Abraham BAUGHAN and Mary Weaver. Minister, Lewis Conner, Baptist. p 7

28 July 1801. Mordecai BAUGHAN and Mary Zimmerman. Minister, Lewis Conner, Baptist. p 8

4 August 1809. John BAYLESS and Fanny Porter. Minister, Lewis Conner, Baptist. p 22

- - -. William BAYLEY and Catherine Smith. Minister, Charles Yates. p 7

17 December 1793. John BAYNE and Sarah Hawkins. Minister, William Mason, Baptist. p 4

22 December 1796. Henry BAYSE and Elizabeth James. Minister, Lewis Corbin. p 6

25 April 1793. Henry BAZEL and Lucy Brandom. Minister, John Koones, Baptist. Green's Notes on Culpeper say Brandon. p 7

19 April 1788. George BEAN and Nancy Petty. Minister, William Mason, Baptist. p 5

11 July 1813. John BECKHAM and Rebecca Gray. Minister, William Mason, Baptist. p 21

4 February 1813. John BEEM and Nancy Bowen. Minister, Lewis Conner, Baptist. p 22

30 November 1815. John BEEM and Patsey Partlow. Minister, Lewis Conner, Baptist. See John Breen. p 23

27 December 1798. Andrew BELTZ and Abigail Retherford. Minister, Reuben Finnell. p 7

21 November 1799. George BENNETT and Mary Holloway. Minister, Frederick Kabler. p 7

5 March 1811. George BENNETT and Peggy Dodson. Minister, Lewis Conner, Baptist. p 22

2 December 1800. John BENNETT and Caty Carder. Minister Absalom Kinsey. p 8

3 February 1786. William BENNETT and Sarah Clatterback. Minister, William Mason, Baptist. p 4

15 November 1792. William BENNETT and Patty Carder. Minister, Lewis Corbin. p 5

11 August 1797. Anthony BERRY and Peggy Ward. Minister, Lewis Conner, Baptist. p 8

15 July 1790. Jesse BERRY and Anna Miller. Minister, William Carpenter, Lutheran. p 6

13 February 1815. Reuben BERRY and Milly Reasons. Minister, William Mason, Baptist. p 22

3 January 1798. William BERRY and Jemimah Weakly. Minister, Lewis Conner, Baptist. p 8

31 December 1807. William BERRY and Lucy Berry. Minister, William Mason, Baptist. p 13

24 November 1790. Simpson BERY (BERRY?) and Jemima Jennett. Minister, William Mason, Baptist. p 6

29 August 1799. John BIGBIE and Sally Wheatlye. Minister, Reuben Finnell. p 7

7 March 1793. Thomas BINGHAM and Nancy Norman. Minister, William Mason, Baptist. p 6

-   -   1796. Joshua BIRKLAND and Frances Harden. Green's Notes on Culpeper. p 59

12 January 1805. Jonathon BISHOP and Nancy Kabler. Minister, John Kabler. p 21

16 October 1798. John BISHOP and Ann Stokes. Minister, William Mason, Baptist. p 5

30 November 1784. Josiah BISHOP and Susanna Inskeep. Minister, John Price, Baptist. p 4

7 March 1794. Thomas BISHOP and Elizabeth Morris. Minister William Mason, Baptist. p 4

17 August 1784. James BLACK and Eleanor Vaughn. Minister, William Mason, Baptist. p 4

20 December 1781. Churchill BLACKEY and Mary Clark. Minister, George Eve, Baptist. p 4

13 October 1789. William BLACKEY and Polly Gaines. Minister, William Carpenter, Lutheran. p 6

16 January 1798. Joseph BLACKWELL and Frances Hopper. Minister, John Hickerson, Baptist. Frances dau. of Thomas Hooper, will 25 January 1803; pro. 20 November 1809. p 6

2 March 1795. William BLACKWELL and Ann Edmonds. Married at Captain Green's by the Rev. John Woodville, Rector of St. Mark's Parish, Episcopal Church. St. Mark's Parish Register.

27 May -. William BLACKWELL and Rachel Tompkins. Minister, John Hickerson, Baptist. p 7

18 June 1815. Thomas BLAIR and Dinah Wood. Minister, William Mason, Baptist. p 22

14 January 1810. William BLAIR and Polly McQueen. Minister, William Mason, Baptist. p 15

22 May 1808. James BLAKE and Sarah Asher. Minister William Fristoe, Baptist. p 21

26 August 1809. John BLAKE and Lucy Atkins. Minister, William Fristoe, Baptist. p 21

1 February 1791. Jacob BLANKENBIKER and Hannah Weaver. Minister, William Carpenter, Lutheran. Tax list says Blankenbecker. Culpeper Minute Book 1763-1764 Says Blankenbeker. Green's Notes on Culpeper says Blackenbaker. p 6

27 July 1790. James BLAKENBIKER and Elizabeth Carpenter. Minister, William Carpenter, Lutheran. p 6

22 February 1791. Samuel BLAKENBIKER and Charlotte Leatherer. Minister, William Carpenter, Lutheran. p 6

- - 1781. Churchill BLAKEY and Mary Clark. Green's Notes on Culpeper. p 58

- - 1799. William BLAKEY and Polly Gaines. Green's Notes on Culpeper. p 58

30 August 1785. James BLEDSOE and Judith Ward. Minister, George Eve, Baptist. p 3

14 October 1789. Thomas BOHANNON and Frances Dicken. Minister, William Mason, Baptist. p 5

17 January 1792. Joel BOLING and Ann Gaines. Minister, George Eve, Baptist. (Bolling). p 5

26 January 1792. William BONIFIELD and ELizabeth Wilson. Minister, William Wright. p 3

9 February 1804. John BOOKER and Kitty Taliaferro. Minister, William Carpenter, Lutheran. p 11

24 January 1786. John BOOTON and Frances Clark. Minister, George Eve, Baptist. p 3

26 November 1798. Joseph B. BOTTS and Nancy Fristoe. Minister, William Fristoe, Baptist. p 7

30 March 1791. William BOTTS and Ann Gaines. Minister, William Mason, Baptist. p 6

26 February 1793. Henry BOUGHAN and Elizabeth Wall. Minister, William Mason, Baptist. p 6

7 December 1788. Francis BOWEN and Milly Yates. Minister, William Mason, Baptist. p 5

6 January 1814. James BOWEN and Ann Foushee. Minister, William Mason, Baptist. p 22

6 November 1815. James BOWEN and Amelia Pollard. Minister, William
Mason, Baptist. p 23

7 March 1797. Joseph BOWEN and Nancy Gibson. Minister, Nathaniel
Sanders, Baptist. p 5

8 June 1815. Peter B. BOWEN and Sarah Fishback. Minister, William
Mason, Baptist. p 22

25 May 1815. William BOWEN and Polly Partlow. Minister, Lewis Conner,
Baptist. p 22

12 January 1810. George BOWLING and ELizabeth Priest. Minister, Lewis
Conner, Baptist. p 22

23 December 1788. Jesse BOWLING and Nancy Kelly. Minister, John Pickett,
Baptist. p 4

20 January 1810. Henry BOWYER and Rebecca Bennett. Minister, Absolem
King. p 20

7 September 1804. Joseph BRADFORD and Lucy Edwards. Minister, Charles
Yates. p 21

6 February 1806. William BRADFORD and Nancy Fry. Minister, William
Carpenter, Lutheran. p 15

13 November 1788. Augustin BRADLEY and Frankey Hurt. Minister, William
Carpenter, Lutheran. p 3

26 February 1805. Augustine BRADLEY and Polly Lillard. Minister, Lewis
Conner, Baptist. p 18

7 March 1799. John BRADY and Rosamond Butt. Minister, Absolom Kinsey.
p 7

11 March 1809. Evans BRAGG and Polly Hudson. Minister, Lewis Conner,
Baptist. p 22

27 September 1802. Ezekiel BRAGG and Nancy Estes. Minister, Frederick
Kabler. p 8

12 October 1800. Gabriel BRAGG and Polly Estes. Minister, Charles Yates.
p 7

4 September 1785. Benjamin BRAGGS and Polly Twentimen. Minister, John
Price, Baptist. p 4

12 May 1784. James BRANHAM and Betty Doggett. Minister, William Mason,
Baptist. p 4

9 February 1806. James BRANHAM and Margaret Lindsey. Minister, Isham
Tatum. p 12

19 February 1789. John BRANHAM and Sally Boswell. Minister, William
Mason, Baptist. p 5

6 October 1797. Nimrod BRANHAM and Peggy Marshall. Minister, William
Mason, Baptist. p 5

4 October 1798. Reuben BRANHAM and Becca Farler. Minister, Charles Yates.
Green's Notes on Culpeper say Farley. p 6

29 January 1798. Richard BRANHAM and Margaret Threlkeld. Minister,
William Mason, Baptist. p 5

19 December 1784. William BRANHAM and Elizabeth Yates. Minister,
William Mason, Baptist. p 4

30 November 1806. Daniel BRANNIN and Elizabeth Canaday. Minister,
William Mason, Baptist. p 13

20 December 1807. Vinson BRANSON and Anna Dodson. Minister, Lewis
Conner, Baptist. p 19

19 January 1808. James BRANY and Charity Humphrey. Minister, William
Mason, Baptist. p 13

6 March 1802. William BREEDLOVE and Margaret Wright. Minister, Frederick
Kabler. p 8

1 November 1793. Ananias BREEDWELL and Calay Daniel. Minister, John
Pickett, Baptist. Green's Notes on Culpeper say Celey. p 3

30 November 1815. John BREEN and Patsey Partlow. Minister, Lewis
Conner, Baptist. See John Breem. p 23

7 March 1796. Cuthbert BRIDWELL and Mary Hilton. Minister, William
Mason, Baptist. p 5

-   -   1782. James BRIANT and Susannah Jollett. Green's Notes on
Culpeper. p 58

4 June 1782. James BRIENT and Susanna Jollett. Minister, George Eve,
Baptist. p 3

27 December 1797. James BRIGHT and Dinah Johnston. Minister, John
Hickerson, Baptist. p 6

1 January 1804. John BRISCO and Maria Horner. Minister, Reuben Finnell.
p 11

28 December 1815. John BRITTON and Polly Bragg. Minister, Lewis Conner, Baptist. p 23

3 March 1792. Thomas BROADUS and Susanna White. Minister, William Mason, Baptist. p 3

8 December 1804. Christopher BROFY and Clara Halor. Minister, Reuben Finnell. p 14

- - 1792. William BROOKE and Fannie Lloyd. Green's Notes on Culpeper. p 58

27 December 1792. William BROOKS and Fanny Loyd. Minister, George Eve, Baptist. p 5

20 February 1792. Armistead BROWN and Peggy Collins. Minister, William Mason, Baptist. p 3

13 January 1804. Braxton BROWN and Lucy Carder. Minister, William Mason, Baptist. p 9

9 October 1794. Charles BROWN and Nancy Hall. Minister, William Mason, Baptist. p 5

30 January 1794. Daniel BROWN and Peggy Covington. Minister, William Mason, Baptist. p 4

- - 1809. Daniel BROWN and Penelope Collins. Minister, Abraham Kersey. p 12

1 August 1805. Enoch BROWN and Sally Yates. Minister, Charles Yates. p 21

22 December 1802. Evan BROWN and Mary Ann Williams. Minister, Frederick Kabler. p 8

11 August 1784. Garfield BROWN and Nancy Long. Minister, Isham Tatum. p 3

16 January 1798. Henry P. BROWN and Hannah Butler. Minister, John Swindler. p 6

26 April 1786. Hezekiah BROWN and Sarah Long. Minister, Nathaniel Sanders, Baptist. p 4

22 July 1788. James BROWN and Elizabeth Gore. Minister, Nathaniel Sanders, Baptist. p 4

12 April 1791. James BROWN and Suckey Zimmerman. Minister, William Mason, Baptist. p 6

20 December 1803. James BROWN and Sally Jett. Minister, Reuben Finnell. p 11

1 November 1804. James BROWN and Mary Smith. Minister, Lewis Conner, Baptist. p 17

23 December 1806. James BROWN and Cassandra Mennefee. Minister, Lewis Conner, Baptist. p 19

7 October 1814. James BROWN and Kelly Morris. Minister, William Mason, Baptist. p 22

7 August 1787. John BROWN and Phoebe Brown. Minister, William Mason, Baptist. p 5

23 January 1795. John BROWN and Polly Norman. Minister, William Mason, Baptist. p 5

26 September 1804. John BROWN and Caty Ramey. Minister, Charles Yates. p 21

11 January 1812. John BROWN, Jr., and Lucy Hughes. Minister, John Owen. p 21

28 January 1808. John J. BROWN and Susannah Dulany. Minister, William Mason, Baptist. p 13

15 March 1809. John H. BROWN and Sarah Hill. Minister, William Carpenter, Lutheran. p 21

12 February 1811. John Powell BROWN and Isabella Thompson. Minister, Lewis Conner, Baptist. p 22

29 August 1799. Nicholas BROWN and Nancy Cardwell. Minister, Frederick Kabler. p 7

8 March 1796. Thomas BROWN and Elener Weatherall. Minister, William Mason, Baptist. Green's Notes on Culpeper say Eleanor. p 5

23 December 1814. Thomas C. BROWN and Frances H. Griffin. Minister, Lewis Conner, Baptist. p 22

9 February 1786. William BROWN and Lucy Campbell. Minister, William Mason, Baptist. p 4

19 January 1798. William BROWN and Mary C - . Minister, Frederick Kabler. p 8

8 January 1807. William BROWN and Mary Griffin. Minister, William Mason, Baptist. p 13

17 March 1814. William BROWN and Tabitha R. Menefee. Minister, Lewis Conner, Baptist. p 22

- - - . Caleb BROWNING and Anna Moore. Minister, John Pickett, Baptist. p 4

21 March 1793. Francis BROWNING and Polly Farmer. Minister, John Hickerson, Baptist. p 7

15 October 1802. Francis BROWNING and Polly Yates. Minister, Frederick Kabler. p 8

25 December 1809. George BROWNING and Gillean Covington. Minister, Lewis Conner, Baptist. p 22

28 February 1789. James BROWNING and Jane Whitledge. Minister, John Pickett, Baptist. p 4

29 May 1798. John BROWNING and Frances Pendleton. Minister, William Mason, Baptist. p 5

25 December 1800. Nicholas BROWNING and Lucy Browning. Minister, James Garnett, Baptist. p 10

20 March 1794. Shadrack BROWNING and Peggy Routt. Minister, William Mason, Baptist. p 4

25 October 1792. Taliaferro BROWNING and Mary Browning. Minister, John Pickett, Baptist. p 7

29 October 1793. Thomas BROWNING and Elizabeth Sewright. Minister, John Pickett, Baptist. p 3

28 December 1793. Thomas BROWNING and Elizabeth Bywaters. Minister, John Pickett, Baptist. p 3

26 December 1792. William BROWNING and Lucy McClanahan. Minister, William Carpenter, Lutheran. p 6

27 June 1793. William BROWNING and Nancy Stone. Minister, Lewis Corbin. p 6

10 September 1789. Benjamin BRUCE and Mary Crisal. Minister, Willliam Mason, Baptist. p 5

12 January 1810. Elijah BRUCE and Malinda Browning. Minister, Lewis Conner, Baptist. p 22

11 October 1799. Ignatius BRUCE and Sinah Johnston. Minister, John Hickerson, Baptist. Green's Notes on Culpeper say Sarah. p 7

19 December 1786. James BRUCE and Lucracia Gaines. Minister, William Mason, Baptist. p 4

1 July 1793. John BRUMLEY and Martha Harper. Minister, John Pickett, Baptist. Green's Notes on Culpeper say Hopper. p 3

4 February 1804. James BRYAN and Lotty Kennard. Minister, Charles Yates. p 9

16 July 1807. John BRYAN and Nancy Lillard. Minister, Lewis Conner, Baptist. p 19

18 February 1783. Thomas BRYAN and Mary Stanton. Minister, George Eve, Baptist. p 4

24 August 1784. John Henry BUCK and Lucy Colvin. Minister, William Mason, Baptist. p 5

27 August 1797. John BUCKHANNON and Sarah Jones. Minister, Frederick Kabler. Cul Min. Bk. 1763-1764 says Buchannon. Green's Notes on Culpeper say Buckannon. p 7

19 May 1814. Bailey BUCKNER and Mildred Strother. Minister, Lewis Conner, Baptist. p 22

29 October 1813. Charles BULLARD and Martha W. Herndon. Minister, William Mason, Baptist. p 21

6 March 1788. John BURDINE and Jemima Clark. Minister, George Eve, Baptist. Green's Notes on Culpeper say Burdyne. p 3

9 January 1815. Alexander BURGESS and Agnes Reece. Minister, Lewis Conner, Baptist. p 22

14 January 1802. William BURK and Nancy Weaver. Minister, William Mason, Baptist. p 8

16 March 1797. Edmund BURKE and Frances Weaver. Minister, William Mason, Baptist. p 5

25 June 1805. John BURKE and Betsey Berry. Minister, Lewis Conner, Baptist. p 18

27 October 1796. Joshua BURKLAND and Frances Harden. Minister, John Swindler. p 5

- - 1799. Reuben BURLY and Jeannetta Delaney. Green's Notes on Culpeper. See Reuben Busley. p 59

2 August 1812. Harris BURNS and Nancy Hudson. Minister, Lewis Conner, Baptist. p 22

6 November 1803. Thomas BURRAS and Polly Meade. Minister, Lewis Conner, Baptist. p 17

25 December 1799. Reuben BUSLEY and Jennetta Delaney. Minister, John Hickerson, Baptist. See Reuben Burley. p 7

23 December 1801. Aaron BUTLER and Sarah Sims. Minister, William Mason, Baptist. Sarah, dau. Richard Sims, Will 16 April 1809; pro. 19 June 1809. p 8

6 December 1801. Armistead BUTLER and Mary Wheatly. Minister, Reuben Finnell. p 11

1 December 1790. Benjamin BUTLER and Mary Edwards. Minister, John Pickett, Baptist. p 7

12 November 1809. Charles BUTLER and Susanna Neale. Minister, Lewis Conner, Baptist. p 22

26 January 1798. Elijah BUTLER and Catherine Watts. Minister, Frederick Kabler. p 29

26 December 1805. John BUTLER and Nancy Butler. Minister, Reuben Finnell. p 14

28 December 1804. Taliafero BUTLER and Janny Grimsley. Minister, Lewis Conner, Baptist. p 17

30 November 1813. Taliaferro BUTLER and Polly Miller. Minister, Lewis Conner, Baptist. p 22

- - -. Towson BUTLER and Catherine Blackwell. Minister, John Hickerson, Baptist. p 7

- - 1796. William BUTLER and Elizabeth Green. Green's Notes on Culpeper. p 59

29 November 1805. William BUTLER and Tabatha Settle. Minister, Lewis Conner, Baptist. p 18

20 March 1800. John BUTT and Elizabeth Morris. Minister, William Mason, Baptist. p 7

22 September 1803. Samuel BUTT and Nancy Oder. Minister, Lewis Conner, Baptist. p 17

11 February 1806. Thomas N. BUTT and Caty G. Broadus. Minister, William Mason, Baptist. p 16

19 April 1796. William BUTT and Elizabeth Green. Minister, William Mason, Baptist. p 5

8 January 1793. James BUTTERFIELD and Polly Ballinger. Minister, William Mason, Baptist. p 6

20 October 1812. Martin BUTTON and Catherine Matthews. Minister, George Simms. p 21

1 June 1792. Frederick CABLER and Anne Threlkeld. Minister, William Mason, Baptist. Green's Notes on Culpeper say Cobler. This must be Kabler; no Cabler in tax list. See Frederick Kabler. p 24

7 August 1785. Zachary CAGHILL and Alice McGannon. Minister, Nathaniel Sanders, Baptist. Minute Book gives Zachary Cogwell. Both names in Culpeper County. p 24

2 January 1805. Philip CALENDAR and Malinda Yancy. Minister, Reuben Finnell. p 14

20 November 1797. Cecilius CALVERT and Nancy (Anne) Beck Calvert, dau. George and Lydia Beck (Ralls) Calvert; b. 1773 d. 1835. He was son of John and Sarah (Bailey 1st wife) Clavert; b. 1767 d. 1852. They were 1st cousins. Minister Charles Yates. Culpeper Marriage Reg. Vol. 1 p 31. Md. Hist. Mag. Vol. 16 p. 195. p 27

17 October 1809. George CALVERT, Jr., and Nancy (Jennings) Norman. Minister, Lewis Conner, Baptist. George Calvert b. 1771, son of George and Lydia Beck (Ralls) Calvert, m. 7 February 1764. p 29

10 May 1809. Jesse CALVERT and Lucey Read or Rea. Minister, Lewis Conner, Baptist. Green's Notes on Culpeper say Seriey Rea - 1810. p 29

28 April 1799. John CALVERT and Sarah Adams. Minister, Charles Yates. p 24

3 February 1804. John CALVERT and Ann Askins. Minister, Reubin Finnell. John Calvert b. 1777 son of George and Lydia Beck (Ralls) Calvert, m. 7 February 1764. p 11

15 November 1790. Ralls CALVERT and Polly Strother. Minister, John Pickett, Baptist. Son of George and Lydia Beck (Ralls) Calvert. M. 7 February 1764. He was b. 1767 and d. 1815. M. Mary Wade Strother dau. Capt. John and Anne (Strother) Strother. (Md. Hist. Mag. Vol. 16 p 198). p 27

12 December 1793. Benjamin CALVIN and Nancy Coleman. Minister, William Mason, Baptist. p 25

9 May 1805. John CAMARON and Esther Olive. Minister, Frederick Kabler. p 21

4 October 1811. Daniel CAMERON and Sally Oliver. Minister, Lewis Conner, Baptist. p 29

30 November 1787. Owen CAMMEL and Jemima Lear. Minister, William Mason, Baptist. Tax list says Campbell. See Owen Campbell. p 25

19 June 1794. Ambrose CAMP and Elizabeth Cowne. Married at Mr. Augustine Cowne's. Minister, Rev. John Woodville, Rector of St. Mark's Parish, Episcopal Church. p 26

- - 1795. Ambrose CAMP and Elizabeth Conner. Green's Notes on Culpeper. p 59

4 August 1803. Ambrose CAMP and Nancy Pierce. Minister, William Mason, Baptist. p 9

- - 1803. Antram CAMP and Nancy Pierce. This must be Ambrose Camp. Green's Notes on Culpeper. p 59

21 November 1805. Marshall CAMP and Lucy Wilkerson. Minister, William Mason, Baptist. p 15

20 December 1798. Willis CAMP and Nancy Colvin. Minister, William Mason, Baptist. p 28

10 March 1796. Elias CAMPBELL and Chloe Swindler. Minister, John Swindler. p 25

5 December 1799. Elijah CAMPBELL and Elizabeth Cannon. Minister, Lewis Conner, Baptist. According to the 1783 tax list there were two Elijah Campbells, Sr. and Jr. in Culpeper. p 28

29 May 1798. John CAMPBELL and Frances Green. Minister, William Mason, Baptist. p 25

16 May 1793. Joseph CAMPBELL and Susanna Shackelford. Minister, John Swindle. p 25

16 May 1807. Morgan CAMPBELL and Mary Huffman. Minister, Lewis Conner, Baptist. p 19

- - 1787. Owen CAMPBELL and Jemima Lear. See Owen Cammel. Green's Notes on Culpeper. p 59

27 December 1789. Patrick CAMPBELL and Lydia Hill. Minister, James Garnett, Baptist. p 26

25 December 1801. Reuben CAMPBELL and Mary Cannon. Minister, Lewis Conner, Baptist. p 28

23 May 1794. Robert CAMPBELL and Lucy Campbell. Minister, John Swindler. p 26

9 December 1791. Silas CAMPBELL and Nancy Turner. Minister, Nathaniel Sanders, Baptist. p 27

24 January 1800. William CAMPBELL and Ann Woodward. Minister, Charles Yates. Called Nancy in family Bible. p 28

29 February 1792. Joel CAMPER and Anna Coons. Minister, John Pickett, Baptist. p 27

2 January 1791. John CAMPER and Susanna Huffman. Minister, William Carpenter, Lutheran. p 27

1 December 1782. Leroy CANADA and Sarah Leavell. Minister, George Eve, Baptist. p 24

28 March 1789. Merida CANNADA and Sally Smoote. Minister, George Eve, Baptist. p 24

27 February 1812. James CANNON and Sarah Scott. Minister, Lewis Conner, Baptist. p 29

9 August 1813. John CANNON, Jr., and Judith Monroe. Minister, Lewis Conner, Baptist. p 29

3 January 1812. Randolph D. CARDEN and Fanny Pierce. Minister, William Mason, Baptist. p 29

7 September 1796. Benjamin CARDER and Polly Carder. Minister, Lewis Colvin. p 26

30 October 1805. Birkett CARDER and Nancy Hawkins. Minister, Lewis Conner, Baptist. Green's Notes on Culpeper say Burkett. p 18

9 April 1799. George CARDER and Letty Brown. Minister, Absalom Kinsey. Green's Notes on Culpeper say Lilly. p 28

12 December 1806. George CARDER and Anne Hume. Minister, Lewis Conner, Baptist. p 19

15 March 1807. William CARDER and Sythia Yowell. Minister, Lewis Conner, Baptist. p 19

9 November 1815. William J. CARDER and Elizabeth Holland. Minister, Lewis Conner, Baptist. p 30

21 January 1793. David CARMICLE and Nancy Anderson. Minister, John Swindler. (Carmichael). p 25

15 June 1802. John CARNAGIE and Frances Jones. Minister, Absalom King. Green's Notes on Culpeper say Carnegie. p 29

11 January 1791. Andrew CARPENTER and Anna Mag Mayland. Minister, William Carpenter, Lutheran. p 27

19 December 1792. Andrew CARPENTER and Elizabeth Kanslar. Minister, William Carpenter, Lutheran. p 26

21 May 1800. Benjamin CARPENTER and Susanna Burks. Minister, William Carpenter, Lutheran. p 28

29 December 1790. Joshua CARPENTER and Leah Smith. Minister, William Carpenter, Lutheran. Green's Notes on Culpeper say Sarah. p 27

26 March 1793. Samuel CARPENTER and Peggy Blankenbaker. Minister, William Carpenter, Lutheran. p 26

17 October 1783. Garland CARR and Mary Phillips. Minister, William Mason, Baptist. p 25

28 December 1797. Charles CARTER and Susanna Tapp. Minister, John Hickerson, Baptist. p 26

28 July 1797. Frederick CARTER and Nancy Jenkins. Minister, Lewis Conner, Baptist. p 28

16 November 1815. Landon CARTER and Polly Lillard. Minister, Lewis Conner, Baptist. p 30

1 March 1803. Thomas CARTER and Margaret Green. Minister, William Mason, Baptist. p 28

5 March 1789. William CARTER and Mary Chester. Minister, John Pickett, Baptist. p 25

26 February 1795. William CARTER and Susanna Googe. Minister, John Swindler. Green's Notes on Culpeper say George. p 26

13 September 1812. William CARTER and Keziah Tannehill. Minister, Lewis Conner, Baptist. p 29

8 December 1789. John CASON and Judith Roebuck. Minister, George Eve, Baptist. p 27

8 January 1789. Edward CASSON and Sally Muse Cave. Minister, George Eve, Baptist. p 24

-    -   1791. Hemp CATLETT and Sallie Pierce. See Kemp Catlett. Green's Notes on Culpeper. p 59

16 June 1791. Kemp CATLETT and Sally Pierce. Minister, William Mason, Baptist. See Hemp Catlett. p 24

16 August 1791. Joseph CAVE and Mary Jenkins. Minister, William Mason,
Baptist. p 24

29 January 1782. Reuben CAVE and Anne Jenkins. Minister, George Eve,
Baptist. p 24

16 April 1801. William CAVE and Susanna Fincham. Minister, Lewis
Conner, Baptist.

4 March 1784. Dudley CHACKELFORD and Winifred Waterspon. Minister,
William Mason, Baptist. Tax list gives Dudley Shackelford. See
Dudley Shackelford. p 25

5 January 1798. Cadwallader CHAPMAN and Polly Morris. Minister, Charles
Yates. p 27

6 January 1785. Erasmus CHAPMAN and Nancy Lewis. Minister, William
Mason, Baptist. p 25

18 August 1800. Henry CHAPMAN and Elizabeth Morris. Minister, Charles
Yates. p 28

14 February 1797. John CHAPMAN and Elizabeth Menefee. Minister, Charles
Yates. p 27

9 August 1799. Zachariah CHAPPALEAR and Linney Settle. Minister, John
Pickett, Baptist. p 28

21 August 1806. Elijah CHEEK and Milly Horton. Minister, Lewis Conner,
Baptist. p 18

1 January 1801. Francis CHEEK and Nancy Gaines. Minister, Lewis Conner,
Baptist. p 28

31 January 1793. George CHEEK and Elizabeth Williams. Minister, John
Swindler. p 25

21 May 1809. James CHEEK and Nancy Harlan. Minister, Lewis Conner,
Baptist. Green's Notes on Culpeper say Horton. p 29

25 December 1787. Elias CHELF and Elizabeth Weaver. Minister, William
Carpenter, Lutheran. p 24

12 July 1792. John CHEWNING and Tabitha Reed. Minister, Lewis Colvin.
Tabitha dau. John Read, will 21 September 1819; pro. 19 June 1820.
p 26

6 February 1807. George CHILTON and Elenor Zimmerman. Minister, William
Mason, Baptist. p 13

2 May 1809. George CHILTON and Sally Asher. Minister, Lewis Conner,
Baptist. p 29

20 October 1796. Richard CHILTON and Sarah Shirer (?). Minister, Lewis
Conner, Baptist. Green's Notes on Culpeper say Sarah Short.

19 August 1790. Stephen CHILTON and Frances Norman. Minister, Isham
Tatum. p 27

9 June 1791. William CHISHAM and Delphia Raines. Minister, Nathaniel
Sanders, Baptist. p 25

1 April 1790. Robert CHOWNING and Mildred Walker. Minister, John
Pickett, Baptist. Green's Notes on Culpeper say Chewning. p 27

3 January 1793. Christopher CHRIGLER and Nancy Botts. Minister, William
Mason, Baptist. See Christopher Crigler. p 26

5 May 1791. Jeremiah CHRISEL and Mary Bruce. Minister, William Mason,
Baptist. p 26

7 April 1799. James CHRISTENBERRY and Elizabeth Threlkeld. Minister,
William Mason, Baptist. p 28

2 February 1803. John CHRISTIAN and Ann Powell. Minister, Frederick
Kabler. p 8

20 December 1792. Abraham CHRISTLER and Nancy Harvey. Minister, William
Carpenter, Lutheran. Green's Notes on Culpeper say Mary. p 26

12 August 1792. Julius CHRISTLER and Elizabeth Souther. Minister,
William Carpenter, Lutheran. Green's Notes on Culpeper say Julian.
p 25

27 July 1786. John CLARK and Milly Gibbs. Minister, George Eve, Baptist.
p 24

13 December 1798. Josias CLARK and Jane Adams. Minister, Reuben Finnal.
p 25

8 November 1791. Robert CLARK and Joannah Jones. Minister, James
Garnett, Baptist. p 25

5 February 1801. Thomas CLARK and Tomsey Powell. Minister, Frederick
Kabler. p 28

29 December 1791. William CLARK and Lucretia Clark. Minister, George
Eve, Baptist. p 25

13 September 1813. William CLARKE and Julia Jenkins. Minister, Lewis
Conner, Baptist. p 29

19 December 1799. Gabriel CLATTERBUCK and Nancy Richardson. Minister,
Lewis Conner, Baptist. p 28

20 June 1809. Landon CLATTERBACK and Nelly Ross. Minister, James Garnett, Baptist. p 15

13 January 1786. James CLATTERBUCK and Elizabeth Hunt. Minister, John Price, Baptist. Green's Notes on Culpeper say Hurt. p 25

3 May 1792. William CLATTERBUCK and Dicy Turner. Minister, James Garnett, Baptist. p 27

17 January 1798. George CLAYTON and Elizabeth Gaines. Minister, Isham Tatum. Elizabeth, dau. Richard Gaines will 4 February 1807; pro. 16 February 1807. p 27

6 August 1807. Thomas CLAYTON and Sarah Cunningham. Minister, Reuben Finnell. p 15

10 January 1799. Aaron CLEMENTS and Lucy Shackelford. Minister, Absalom Kinsey. p 28

2 September 1799. Philip CLINE and Polly Turner. Minister, Frederick Kabler. p 27

24 December 1790. Aarlon CLORE and Susanna Swindler. Minister, William Mason, Baptist. p 26

24 December 1790. Benjamin CLORE and Anne Christopher. Minister, William Mason, Baptist. p 26

2 March 1792. Samuel CLORE and Frances Christopher. Minister, William Mason, Baptist. p 24

3 December 1791. William COCHIN (Cochran) and Charity Spencer. Minister, John Pickett, Baptist. p 27

22 December 1790. John COCK and Martha Powell. Minister, George Eve, Baptist. Green's Notes on Culpeper say Cook. p 27

20 October 1796. Henry COCKS and Susanna Mills. Minister, Frederick Kabler. p 27

29 June 1803. Matthew COGHILL and Betsey Hisel (Hisle). Minister, Charles Yates. p 9

16 August 1795. John COHILL and Eleanor Butts. Minister, Lewis Conner, Baptist. p 26

12 January 1797. Josias COLBERT and Susanna Spiller. Minister, John Swindler. p 25

29 March 1798. Farish COLEMAN and Elizabeth Camp. Minister, William Mason, Baptist. p 25

15 March 1798. Jeremiah COLES and Mary Shepherd. Minister, Frederick Kablar. p 29

31 August 1793. Ambrose COLLINS and Mary Walker. Minister, John Pickett, Baptist. p 24

4 February 1795. Andrew COLLINS and Elizabeth Freeman. Married at Robert Freeman's by Rev. John Woodville, Rector of St. Mark's Parish, Episcopal Church. Elizabeth, dau. Robert Freeman, will 31 July 1811; pro. 15 September 1811. p 26

7 April 1813. Andrew COLLINS and Polly Morris. Minister, William Mason, Baptist. p 29

28 February 1793. John COLLINS and Charlotte Wortham. Minister, William Mason, Baptist. p 26

10 November 1807. William COLLINS and Avie Sims. Minister, William Mason, Baptist. Avie, dau. Richard Sims, will 16 April 1809; pro. 19 June 1809. p 13

19 May 1812. John COLSOLVER and Anne Blair. Minister, William Mason, Baptist. p 29

20 November 1797. Cornelius COLVERT and Nancy Colvert. Minister, Charles Yates. See Cornelius Calvert. p 27

2 April 1801. Gabriel COLVIN and Polly Roberts. Minister, William Mason, Baptist. p 28

13 November 1806. James COLVIN and Polly Hill. Minister, William Mason, Baptist. Polly, dau. William Hill, will 25 January 1809; pro. 20 April 1812. Called Patsey in will. p 13

25 December 1806. Jeremiah COLVIN and Sally Smith. Minister, William Mason, Baptist. p 13

27 October 1789. John COLVIN and Elizbeth Colvin. Minister, William Mason, Baptist. p 25

24 April 1788. Mason COLVIN and Elizabeth Hawkins. Minister, William Mason, Baptist. p 25

14 February 1815. Robert COLVIN and Patty Yeager. Minister, William Mason, Baptist. p 30

23 December 1800. Daniel COMPTON and Betsey Yates. Minister, James Garnett, Baptist. p 10

10 January 1799. Edward COMPTON and Rebecca Murphy. Minister, Reuben Finnell. p 27

23 January 1800. Howard COMPTON and Elizabeth Yates. Minister, Charles Yates. p 28

23 December 1806. Matthew COMPTON and Nancy Vaughan. Minister, Lewis Conner, Baptist. p 19

21 February 1792. Samuel COMPTON and Elizabeth Harper. Minister, Willial Wright. p 24

16 September 1802. Stephen COMPTON and Elener Duke. Minister, Reuben Finnell. p 11

16 February 1798. Walter COMPTON and Elizabeth Adams. Minister, John Pickett, Baptist. p 28

27 February 1802. William COMPTON and Anna Hay. Minister, Reuben Finnell. p 11

16 December 1796. John CONNER and Nancy Wigginton. Minister, William Mason, Baptist. p 26

15 December 1796. Uriel CONNER and Nancy Nalle. Minister, William Mason, Baptist. p 25

14 December 1815. Alfred COOKE and Susannah Corbin. Minister, William Mason, Baptist. p 30

23 July 1794. George COOKE and Elizabeth Stipe. Minister, Frederick Kabler. p 27

14 April 1793. Lewis COOKE and Mary Yager. Minister, William Carpenter, Lutheran. p 26

23 March 1799. Philip COOKE and Sally Doggett. Minister, Frederick Kablar. p 27

6 November 1782. Thomas COOKE and Margaret Debourd. Minister, George Eve, Baptist. p 24

26 April 1804. Thornton P. COOKE and Anne Ward. Minister, Lewis Conner, Baptist. p 17

20 September 1800. William COOKE and Betsy R. Howe. Minister, William Mason, Baptist. p 28

14 January 1788. Frederick COONS and Mary Ann Mathews. Minister, John Pickett, Baptist. p 24

25 November 1791. James COONS and Anne Atwood. Minister, John Hickerson, Baptist. p 26

22 August 1792. John COONS and Ann Coons. Minister, John Hickerson, Baptist. p 26

- - 1808. Leroy COOPER and Harriet Byron Vaughan. Green's Notes on Culpeper. p 161

30 April 1809. Robert COOPER and Nancy Triplett. Minister, William Mason, Baptist. p 16

28 April 1808. William COOPER and Laura Smith. Minister, William Mason, Baptist. Laura, dau. William Smith, will 29 July 1811; pro. 16 September 1811. p 13

15 September 1786. Benjamin CORBIN and Ann Corbin. Minister, John Pickett, Baptist. p 24

24 December 1798. Charles CORBIN and Nancy Jews. Minister, Reuben Finnell. p 27

20 January 1800. Fielding CORBIN and Susanna Collins. Minister, Charles Yates. p 28

15 December 1814. George CORBIN and Sally Monroe. Minister, Lewis Conner, Baptist. p 29

15 March 1812. Jameson CORBIN and Mary N. Kearn. Minister, William Mason, Baptist. p 29

10 August 1799. Joseph CORBIN and Hannah Menefee. Minister, Charles Yates. p 24

17 March 1787. Martin CORBIN and Nancy Scott. Minister, John Pickett, Baptist. p 24

12 August 1811. Mechum CORBIN and Nancy Bywaters. Minister, William Mason, Baptist. p 29

3 November 1811. Thomas CORBIN and Elizabeth Johnston. Minister, William Mason, Baptist. p 29

25 December 1792. Elias CORDER and Anna Tapp. Minister, John Pickett, Baptist. p 27

30 March 1792. James CORDER and Sally Googe. Minister, Lewis Colvin. p 26

29 December 1794. Charles CORNELIUS and Elizabeth Jennings. Minister, William Williamson. p 26

17 October 1797. John CORNELIUS and Judith Mason. Minister, William Mason, Baptist. p 26

19 December 1786. William CORNELIUS and Betsy Plunckett. Minister, Thomas Ammon, Baptist. p 24

24 December 1794. Christopher COURTNEY and Mary Ann Johnston. Minister, William Mason, Baptist. p 25

14 November 1793. James COURTNEY and Annes Johnston. Minister, William Mason, Baptist. Bride's name indexed Ames. p 25

9 March 1797. Isaac COWGILL and Elizabeth Stokesbury. Minister, Frederick Kabler. p 28

27 September 1801. John COWGILL and Polly Huans. Minister, Frederick Kabler. p 28

10 October 1800. Thomas COWGILL and Sarah Antrim. Minister, William Mason, Baptist. p 28

2 January 1789. Augustine COWNE and Frances Yancey. Minister, William Mason, Baptist. p 25

29 December 1803. Thomas COWNE and Lucy Gaines. Minister, Reuben Finnell. p 11

15 August 1799. David J. COX and Ann Calvert. Minister, Reuben Finnell. Anne Calvert, dau. John Calvert and his second wife, Helen Bailey. Davis J. Coxe is called Captain. p 28

16 May 1808. Benjamin CRAIG and Betsey Green. Minister, Lewis Conner, Baptist. p 20

11 May 1787. Reuben CRAIGG and Frances Twyman. Minister, George Eve, Baptist. p 24

4 November 1794. Henry CRANK and Mary Ann Haywood. Minister, Henry Fry. p 27

8 November 1804. George CRAVER and Jane Calvert. Minister, Reuben Finnell. Jane Calvert, dau. George and Lydia Beck (Ralls) Calvert. Born 1785. p 12

24 December 1789. Aaron CRAWFORD and Ruth Threlkeld. Minister, William Mason, Baptist. p 26

18 September 1806. Joseph CRAWFORD and Mag Utterback. Minister, Lewis Conner, Baptist. p 18

24 October 1786. Oliver CRAWFORD and Lucy Alexander. Minister, George Eve, Baptist. p 24

31 December 1811. John CREAL and Fanny Kilby. Minister, Lewis Conner, Baptist. p 29

- - 1793. Christopher CRIGLER and Frances Botts. See Christopher Chrigler. Green's Notes on Culpeper. p 61

28 August 1810. James CRIGLER and Sally H. Triplett. Minister, William Mason, Baptist. p 15

11 June 1812. James CRIGLER and Susan W. Gaines. Minister, William Mason, Baptist. p 29

25 December 1789. John CRIGLER and Salley Hume. Minister, Isham Tatum. Original Register. p 32

9 June 1809. Shefley CRIGLER and Leanah Suddith. Minister, Lewis Conner, Baptist. p 29

18 February 1805. William CRIGLER and Kitty Brown. Minister, Reuben Finnell. p 14

28 March 1806. Robert CROOK and Nancy Campbell. Minister, Lewis Conner, Baptist. p 18

17 January 1793. William CROUCH and Mary Crawford. Minister, John Swindler. p 25

10 February 1798. Coleman CRUTCHER and Elizabeth Pierce. Minister, William Mason, Baptist. p 25

13 July 1791. John CUNNINGHAM and Janny Haddox. Minister, John Pickett, Baptist. p 27

23 December 1802. John G. CURRON and Lucy Wall. Minister, Reuben Finnell. p 11

1 April 1806. Elijah CURTIS and Hepsaba Guinn. Minister, William Mason, Baptist. p 16

24 January 1797. Elijah DANIEL and Nancy Cunningham. Minister, Lewis Corbin. p 40

9 July 1793. Thomas DANIEL and Margaret Rosson. Minister, William Mason, Baptist. p 40

2 April 1785. John DAVENPORT and Elizbeth Pierce. Minister, John Price, Baptist. p 4

11 March 1783. Charles DAVIS and Hannah Gaines. Minister, George Eve, Baptist. p 40

20 May 1787. John DAVIS and Frances Ham-. Minister, George Eve, Baptist. p 40

16 April 1807. John DAVIS and Polly Threlkeld. Minister, William Mason, Baptist. p 13

4 January 1815. John DAVIS and Anne Smith. Minister, Lewis Conner, Baptist. p 41

21 November 1804. Benjamin DAWNES and Elizabeth Slaughter. Minister, Lewis Conner, Baptist. p 17

15 October 1799. John DAWSON and Lucy Gosney. Minister, James Garnett, Baptist. p 41

24 November 1789. Thomas DAWSON and Elizabeth Fooshe (Foushee). Minister, John Leland. p 40

12 August 1801. Charles DAY and Susanna Threlkeld. Minister, Frederick Kabler. p 41

23 December 1813. Horatio DAY and Rebecca Pettinger. Minister, William Mason, Baptist. p 41

25 December 1796. John DAY and Susanna Spilman. Married at Captain Spilman's. Minister, Rev. John Woodville, Rector of St. Mark's Parish, Episcopal Church. St. Mark's Parish Register.

14 January 1796. Thomas DAY and Ellis Duval. Minister, William Mason, Baptist. p 40

21 December 1802. John DEALE and Sally Odor. Minister, Absalom King. p 41

12 March 1800. Peter DEALE and Mary Visecarver. Minister, Lewis Conner, Baptist. p 41

28 March 1789. William DEATHERAGE and Mary Maddox. Minister, John Pickett, Baptist. p 41

25 December 1794. John DELANA and Anne Walle. Minister, Lewis Corbin. Tax list says John Delany. Green's Notes on Culpeper say Dulany. p 40

26 April 1792. Abijah DELANY and Nancy Burk. Minister, William Mason, Baptist. Green's Notes on Culpeper say Dulany and Burke. p 40

5 January 1792. Learoy DELANY and Ann Routt. Minister, William Mason, Baptist. Green's Notes on Culpeper say Dulany. p 40

30 April 1809. John DENTON and Elizabeth Hendrick. Minister, William Mason, Baptist. p 16

31 May 1815. Levy DERRY and Hannah Rambottom. Minister, Paul Haskell. p 41

14 July 1791. Christopher DICKENS and Mary Pulliam. Minister, William Mason, Baptist. p 40

1 December 1789. Thomas B. DICKERSON and Elizabeth Amiss. Minister, John Pickett, Baptist. Green's Notes on Culpeper say <u>Dickenson</u>. p 41

11 October 1802. Edward DICKINSON and Elizabeth Landrum. Minister, Frederick Kabler. Green's Notes on Culpeper say <u>Dickenson</u>. p 9

17 September 1800. James DILLARD and Jane Edrington. Minister, John Pickett, Baptist. p 41

10 November 1805. Asa DILLIAN and Lydia Bigbee. Minister, Reuben Finnell. p 14

26 May 1784. John DIVERS and Margaret Collence. Minister, George Eve, Baptist. This name may be Collins. No Collence in Culpeper Tax list and there are 4 or 5 Collins. p 63

24 December 1785. Thomas DOBBS and Sarah Johnston. Minister, Isham Tatum. p 40

1 February 1791. David DODSON and Lucy Hisle. Minister, John Swindler. p 40

30 October 1803. James DODSON and Margaret Woodard. Minister, Charles Yates. p 9

31 October 1805. Joel DODSON and Polly Fincham. Minister, Lewis Conner, Baptist. p 18

23 February 1803. Stephen DODSON and Catherine Chilton. Minister, John Swindler. p 40

2 September 1801. William DODSON and Judith Chilton. Minister, Lewis Conner, Baptist. p 41

17 March 1814. Henry DOGAN and Elizabeth Hilton. Minister, Isham Tatum. p 41

10 December 1788. James DOGGETT and Anne Brown. Minister, Nathaniel Sanders, Baptist. p 4

11 December 1794. Thomas B. DOGGETT and Sally Ward. Minister, Lewis Corbin. p 40

28 September 1802. Thomas DOGGETT and Sarah Hardin. Minister, Frederick Kabler. p 41

9 July 1807. Richard J. DOGGETT and Maria Ward. Minister, Lewis Conner, Baptist. p 19

24 August 1809. Quarles DOSSETT and Lavinia Sisk. Minister, Lewis Conner, Baptist. Green's Notes on Culpeper say <u>Dorsett</u>. p 41

- - 1782. Nehemiah DOWD and Elizabeth Goodman. Green's Notes on Culpeper. p 61

6 February 1782. Nehemiah DOWSELL and Elizabeth Goodman. Minister, George Eve, Baptist. p 40

14 November 1799. Richard DUKE and Elizabeth McDogle. Minister, Reuben Finnell. p 41

- - 1803. Elias DULANY and Fanny McQueen. Minister, Lewis Conner, Baptist. p 17

11 December 1805. Gabriel DULANEY and Patsey Leathers. Minister, Isham Tatum. p 12

4 May 1794. Isaac DUNAWAY and Milly Kinard. Minister, Lewis Conner, Baptist. Green's Notes on Culpeper say Kinnard. p 41

28 February 1793. Benjamin DUNCAN and Elizabeth Browning. Minister, Lewis Corbin. p 40

2 April 1812. Edmund DUNCAN and Harriet Dulaney. Minister, William Mason, Baptist. p 41

17 January 1797. Frederick DUNCAN and Susanna Stallard. Minister, John Hickerson, Baptist. p 40

18 January 1810. George DUNCAN and Hannah Brown. Minister, William Mason, Baptist. p 15

24 December 1805. Gollop DUNCAN and Lucy Covington. Minister, Lewis Conner, Baptist. Gollop Duncan, son of Robert R. Duncan will 7 June 1788; proved 21 October 1793. p 18

27 September 1797. James DUNCAN and Dorcas Butler. Minister, John Swindler. Dorcas, dau. of Spencer Butler, will 20 July 1818; proved 21 September 1818. p 40

24 December 1797. Nimrod DUNCAN and Lucy Browning. Minister, John Swindler. p 40

14 February 1789. William DUNCAN and Lucy Bywaters. Minister, John Pickett, Baptist. p 41

27 April 1802. John DUNKIN and Nancy Browning. Minister, Frederick Kabler. This name may have been Duncan: many Duncans in Culpeper tax list and no Dunkins. p 8

8 March 1814. William DUNNAWAY and Jane Hopkins. Minister, Lewis Conner, Baptist. p 41

23 December 1793. Benjamin DUVAL and Lucy Jennings. Minister, William Mason, Baptist. p 40

21 December 1797. Daniel DUVAL and Polly Herin. Minister, Rev. John Woodville, Rector St. Mark's Parish, Episcopal Church. St. Mark's Parish Register.

18 September 1808. David DYKE and Polly Shaver. Minister, Lewis Conner, Baptist. p 20

26 October 1790. Reuben EARTHEN and Elizabeth Johnston. Minister, John Pickett, Baptist. p 43

4 December 1810. Philip EASTHAM and Polly Farrow. Minister, Lewis Conner, Baptist. p 43

22 November 1808. Benjamin EDDINGS and Fanny Etherton. Minister, William Mason, Baptist. p 16

18 August 1791. Churchill EDDINS and Margaret Hervey. Minister, William Mason, Baptist. Green's Notes on Culpeper say Harvey. p 43

22 October 1789. John EDDINS and Milly Delaney. Minister, George Eve, Baptist. Green's Notes on Culpeper say Dulaney. p 43

19 May 1788. Philip EDWARDS and Easter Corbin. Minister, William Mason, Baptist. p 43

30 December 1785. William EDYER and Martha Lightfoot. Minister, Thomas Ammon, Baptist. See William Edzer. p 43

30 December 1785. William EDZER and Martha Lightfoot. Minister, Thomas Ammon, Baptist. Given both ways, but this is the name that appears in Swem's Index and Edyer does not. Green's Notes on Culpeper say Edgar. p 43

25 July 1800. Payton ELDRIDGE and Polly Guinn. Minister, William Mason, Baptist. p 43

20 December 1804. Augustine ELLIS and Mildred Slaughter. Minister, Lewis Conner, Baptist. p 17

25 December 1803. Owen ELLIS and Margaret McKelbin. Minister, Charles Yates. p 9

18 July 1810. Thomas ELLIS and Amelia Jenkins. Minister, Lewis Conner, Baptist. p 43

9 February 1810. William EMERY and Hannah Patton. Minister, Absolem King.

8 May 1802. Joseph EMRY and Isabel Butler. Minister, Frederick Kabler. p 8

27 October 1799. Charles EMMORY (Emory) and Winney Payton. Minister, Charles Yates. p 43

9 January 1814. Joseph EMMONS and Lucy Latham. Minister, William Mason, Baptist. p 43

21 April 1802. Abraham ESTES and Phebe Peyton. Minister, Frederick Kabler. p 8

7 April 1807. John ESTES and Susanna Butler. Minister, Lewis Conner, Baptist. p 19

26 May 1792. Peter ESTES and Sally Yates. Minister, William Mason, Baptist. p 43

- - -. Samuel ESTES and Mary Peyton. Minister, Charles Yates. p 43

20 March 1800. James ETHERINGTON and Hanah Delaney (Dulaney). Minister, Absolom Kinsey. p 43

6 June 1811. Joseph ETHERTON and Elizabeth T. Sims. Minister, William Mason, Baptist. p 43

19 December 1804. James ETHRINGTON and Martha Blackburn. Minister, Reuben Finnell. p 14

24 January 1799. John ETHERINGTON and Frances Yancey. Minister, Absolom Kinsey. p 43

17 January 1804. Reuben ETHERTON and Elenor McDonald. Minister, William Mason, Baptist. p 9

20 November 1800. John EVANS and Gilly C. Strother. Minister, William Mason, Baptist. p 43

17 June 1786. William EVANS and Betsy Wood. Minister, Thomas Ammon, Baptist. p 43

4 December 1794. Thomas FALCONER and Sally Winston. Married at Mr. Bank's by Rev. John Woodville, Rector of St. Mark's Parish, Episcopal Church. p 44

11 September 1814. Daniel FARMER and Elizbeth L. Dulaney. Minister, William Mason, Baptist. p 45

3 December 1784. John FARMER and Jemima Grant. Minister, William Mason, Baptist. p 44

18 December 1806. William FARROW and Lydia Wiley. Minister, Lewis Conner, Baptist. p 19

17 January 1805. Spencer FAVEL or FEWEL and Lucy Morgan. Minister, Lewis Conner, Baptist. p 18

7 - 1803. John FAYER and Roda Gaines. Minister, Lewis Conner, Baptist. p 17

21 January 1796. William FENCHAM and Elizabeth Clatterbuck. Minister, Lewis Conner, Baptist. p 45

24 August 1793. Abner FENNELL and Nancy Dawling. Minister, William Mason, Baptist. Finnell in tax list also Green's Notes on Culpeper p 62. p 44

25 July 1786. Charles FENNELL and Lucy Fennell. Minister, William Mason, Baptist. Finnell in Green's Notes on Culpeper p 62. p 44

19 February 1795. John FERGUSON and Anne Green. Minister, William Mason, Baptist. p 44

25 January 1811. John FERGUSON and Elizabeth Burton. Minister, William Mason, Baptist. p 45

20 January 1789. Benjamin FEWELL and Nancy Walle. Minister, William Mason, Baptist. p 44

4 January 1798. Benjamin FEWELL and Ann Coghill. Minister, John Swindler. p 44

3 January 1801. James FEWELL and Lucy Zimmerman. Minister, William Mason, Baptist. p 45

14 September 1806. Mason FEWELL and Sarah Fiddle. Minister, Lewis Conner, Baptist. p 18

17 January 1805. Spencer FEWEL or FAVEL and Lucy Morgan. Minister, Lewis Conner, Baptist. p 18

3 March 1787. Benjamin FICKLIN and Susanna Foushee. Minister, William Mason, Baptist. p 44

16 November 1809. Benjamin FINCHAM and Susanna Smith. Minister, Lewis Conner, Baptist. p 45

9 August 1804. William FINCHAM and Betty McAlister. Minister, Lewis Conner, Baptist. p 17

28 February 1815. William FINCHAM and Polly Kebben. Minister, Lewis Conner, Baptist. p 45

27 November 1800. Elijah FINKS and Elizabeth Foster. Minister, William Mason, Baptist. p 45

15 November 1791. Morgan FINNELL and Elizabeth Sisson. Minister, James Garnett, Baptist. p 44

3 October 1788. Jacob FISHBACK and Hannah Huffman. Minister, William Carpenter, Lutheran. p 44

24 October 1804. George FISHER and Dolly Alsop. Minister, Reuben Finnell. p 12

11 August 1803. William FISHER and Polly Hand. Minister, Reuben Finnell. p 11

19 November 1799. John FLEMING and Mary Walle. Minister, Charles Yates. p 44

29 November 1791. Zachariah FLESHMAN and Phoebe Leathers. Minister, William Mason, Baptist. p 44

Before 1781. Francis FLETCHER and Nanny Collins, dau. Thomas Collins. Francis Fletcher's will 25 March 1781, pro. 20 August 1781. Green's Notes on Culpeper. p 48

25 July 1798. James FLETCHER and Edy Bywaters. Minister, John Hickerson, Baptist. p 44

26 July 1801. Rawleigh FLETCHER and Polly Estes. Minister, James Garnett, Baptist. p 10

29 May 1793. Stephen FLETCHER and Mary Barnes. Minister, John Hickerson, Baptist. p 44

11 May 1808. Vinson FLETCHER and Sally Barnes. Minister, William Mason, Baptist. p 13

15 December 1789. John FLOYED (Floyd) and Mary House. Minister, William Carpenter, Lutheran. p 44

29 December 1788. John FLINT and Sally Porter. Minister, Isham Tatum. p 44

17 January 1788. Thomas FLINT and Molly Ballard. Minister, Isham Tatum. p 45

19 January 1788. William FLINT and Elizabeth Ballard. Minister, Isham Tatum. p 45

7 June 1803. Benjamin FORD and Elizabeth F. Leavell. Minister, William Mason, Baptist. p 9

10 April 1788. John FORD and Rosy Nowman. Minister, Isham Tatum. p 45

13 June 1791. Joshua FORD and Nancy Terrell. Minister, James Garnett, Baptist. p 44

9 October 1806. Reuben FORD and Elizabeth Petty. Minister, William Mason, Baptist. p 12

14 March 1805. Robert FOSTER and Elizabeth Finks. Minister, Reuben Finnell. p 14

5 October 1788. John FOUSHEE and Sally Crutcher. Minister, Nathaniel Sanders, Baptist. p 44

- June 1814. Edmund FOX and Betsey Higgason. Minister, William James. p 45

8 April 1787. John FOX and Ann Barber. Minister, William Mason, Baptist. p 44

16 January 1809. William FOX and Mary Woodard. Minister, William Mason, Baptist. p 16

17 January 1788. Jonathan FRANKLIN and Milly Tinsley. Minister, George Eve, Baptist. p 44

4 February 1795. Henry FRAZIER and Nancy Bredlove. Minister, Frederick Kablar. p 44

23 December 1810. John FREEDLOW and Margaret Oder. Minister, Absolem King. p 20

2 March 1813. Garriott FREEMAN and Nancy Foster. Minister, William Mason, Baptist. p 45

4 October 1792. John FREEMAN and Lydia Edge. Minister, Lewis Corbin. p 44

4 February 1806. William FREEMAN and Nancy Hughes. Minister, Lewis Conner, Baptist. p 18

2 November 1786. Ephraim FRY and Mary Huffman. Minister, Isham Tatum. p 44

5 August 1795. John FRY and Debby Haywood. Minister, Isham Tatum. p 45

17 September 1795. Thomas W. FRY and Elizabeth Slaughter. Minister, Isham . p 45

10 January 1788. David FULKS and Elizabeth Huffman. Minister, William Carpenter, Lutheran. p 44

6 March 1782. Samuel FURNIS and Sarah Roberts. Minister, George Eve, Baptist. p 44

10 February 1785. Thomas FURNISH and Frances Denany. Minister, George Eve, Baptist. Furnis in Tax list; Furniss in Green's Notes on Culpeper p 62. p 44

22 November 1791. Abraham GAAR and Dinah Weaver. Minister, William Carpenter, Lutheran. p 47

26 May 1795. Richard Rice GAILOR and Elizabeth Hall "near Fredericksburg". Minister, Rev. John Woodville, Rector of St. Mark's Parish, Episcopal Church. See Richard Rice Sailor. St. Mark's Parish Register.

20 May 1790. David GAINES and Peggy Mitchell. Minister, John Leland. p 46

22 August 1796. Edward W. GAINES and Nancy Yowell. Minister, John Swindler. p 47

15 November 1805. Francis GAINES and Lucy Hughes. Minister, Lewis Conner, Baptist. p 18

18 December 1788. George GAINES and Susanna Graves. Minister, George Eve, Baptist. p 46

12 February 1789. Humphrey GAINES and Elizabeth Warren. Minister, George Eve, Baptist. p 46

20 August 1792. John GAINES and Peggy Wise. Minister, James Garnett, Baptist. p 48

4 May 1789. Richard GAINES and Frances Jolly. Minister, William Mason, Baptist. p 47

25 January 1805. Thomas GAINES and Nancy Fryer. Minister, Lewis Conner, Baptist. p 18

24 November 1799. William P. GAINES and Elizabeth B. Hughes. Minister, Reuben Finnell. p 48

23 February 1793. John GALLAHUE and Anne Rowe. Minister, William Mason, Baptist. p 48

18 December 1785. Lunsford GANT and Sarah Ratliff. Minister, John Pickett, Baptist. p 47

11 August 1807. Edmund GARNER and Susanna Turner. Minister, Lewis Conner, Baptist. p 19

20 June 1787. Edmond GARNETT and Sarah Graves. Minister, George Eve, Baptist. p 47

30 October 1799. Elijah GARNETT and Nancy Branham. Minister, William Mason, Baptist. p 48

29 December 1791. George GARNETT and Sarah Butler. Minister, William Mason, Baptist. p 46

15 November 1791. James GARNETT and Nancy Clark. Minister, James Garnett, Baptist. p 48

8 April 1795. James GARNETT and Molly Jones. Minister, William Mason, Baptist. p 47

23 June 1812. Larkin GARNETT and Elizabeth J. Garnett. Minister, William Mason, Baptist. p 48

4 December 1799. Lawrence GARNETT and Sally Rush. Minister, William Mason, Baptist. p 48

1 April 1790. Robert GARNETT and Eleanor Cockrine. Minister, William Mason, Baptist. Green's Notes on Culpeper say Cochran. p 48

23 October 1792. James GARRIOTT and Susanna Campbell. Minister, Lewis Corbin. p 47

1 May 1800. James GARROTT and Lydia Haynes. Minister, Frederick Kablar. p 48

29 December 1791. John GARRIOTT and Elizabeth Kinnard. Minister, Lewis Corbin. p 47

28 January 1802. Joseph GARRIOTT and Caty Hudson. Minister, Lewis Conner, Baptist. p 48

6 December 1795. Levy GARWOOD and Sarah Inskeep. Minister, William Mason, Baptist. p 47

2 December 1784. Henry GATESKILL and Ann Lightfoot. Minister, William Mason, Baptist. p 47

24 June 1801. Robert GEORGE and Tressey Duncan. Minister, James Garnett, Baptist. p 10

29 October 1789. Zachariah GIBBS and Lucy Clark. Minister, Isham Tatum. p 48

12 August 1801. John GIBSON and Elizabeth Norman. Minister, Frederick Kabler. p 48

4 July 1807. Thomas GIBSON and Nancy Feagins. Minister, Reuben Finnell. p 15

16 January 1787. Samuel GIDDINGS and Sarah Mason. Minister, John Pickett, Baptist. p 47

17 May 1788. Laurence GILLOCK and Betsy Twentiman. Minister, James Garnett, Baptist. p 47

6 January 1785. Lawrence GIN and Sarah Levell. Minister, William Mason, Baptist. p 47

27 February 1787. James GINN and Elizabeth Butt. Minister, William Mason, Baptist. p 47

25 December 1786. Thomas GINN and Elizabeth Grady. Minister, William Mason, Baptist. p 47

9 January 1789. Thomas GINN and Mary Threlkeld. Minister, William Mason, Baptist. p 47

20 November 1798. Ely GLASSCOCK and Susanna Bumgarner (Bumgardner). Minister, Lewis Conner, Baptist. p 48

5 January 1786. George GLORE and Elizabeth Mauck. Minister, Isham Tatum. p 47

20 April 1795. Richard GLOVIER and Milly Shackelford. Minister, John Hickerson, Baptist. p 48

5 January 1790. Lawrence GAAR and Rosanna Broyles. Minister, William Carpenter, Lutheran. p 48

5 March 1807. John GOOCH and Ann Mozingo. Minister, Lewis Conner, Baptist. p 19

4 October 1815. Alexander GORDON, Jr., and Eleanor C. Bell. Minister, Lewis Conner, Baptist. p 54

8 March 1814. James A. GORDEN (Gordon) and Ann G. Gaines. Minister, William Mason, Baptist. p 49

21 September 1809. Mungo M. GORDON and Mildred G. Marye. Minister, Lewis Conner, Baptist. p 48

2 September 1810. William GORDON and Elizabeth Smede. Minister, James Garnett, Baptist. p 21

12 September 1799. William GORE and Mary Sims. Minister, Charles Yates. Green's Notes on Culpeper say Simms. p 47

30 October 1799. William GORE and Mary Sims. Minister, Charles Yates. Both dates given. Green's Notes on Culpeper say Simms. p 48

14 June 1798. Thomas GODFREY and Polly Settle. Minister, John Hickerson, Baptist. p 48

1 September 1799. Enoch GOLDEN and Lucy Googe. Minister, Charles Yates. p 47

23 February 1791. Daniel GOOD and Elizabeth Lipp. Minister, William Carpenter, Lutheran. p 48

18 August 1785. Richard GOODALL and Elizabeth Merry. Minister, George Eve, Baptist. p 47

2 March 1789. Benjamin GOSNEY and Sarah Applebee. Minister, Isham Tatum. p 47

11 April 1800. Richard GOSNEY and Fanny Rowe. Minister, James Garnett, Baptist. p 48

26 July 1795. George GRADY and Fanny Breadlove. Minister, Frederick Kabler. p 48

22 May 1792. Daniel GRAVES and Eleanor Grady. Minister, Nathaniel Sanders, Baptist. p 48

23 December 1788. John GRAVES and Elizabeth Eddins. Minister, George Eve, Baptist. p 46

1 January 1800. Joseph GRAVES and Nelly Branham. Minister, Isham Tatum. p 48

9 January 1794. Leonard GRAVES and Rebecca Bingham. Minister, George Sims. p 46

22 September 1785. Philip GRAVES and Elizabeth Jones. Minister, Isham Tatum. p 46

20 November 1795. Thomas GRAVES, Jr., and Mary Mason. Minister, Lewis Corbin. p 48

2 June 1811. Hezekiah GRAY and Anne Dyke. Minister, Lewis Conner, Baptist. p 49

24 November 1796. Joseph GRAY and Lydia Stout. Minister, William Mason, Baptist. p 47

9 July 1812. John S. GREEN and Lavinia Jett. Minister, Lewis Conner, Baptist. p 49

7 May 1811. Richard GREEN and Elizabeth Haynie. Minister, Lewis Conner, Baptist. p 49

20 January 1812. Thomas GREEN and Mary Hawkins. Minister, William Mason, Baptist. p 48

23 March 1786. Zachariah GRIFFIN and Fanny Hill. Minister, William Mason, Baptist. p 47

26 January 1792. Zachariah GRIFFIN and Clary Nalle. Minister, William Mason, Baptist. p 46

18 March 1808. Henry GRIGSBY and Jany Scott. Minister, Lewis Conner, Baptist. p 20

13 October 1796. John GRIGSBY and Susanna Jones. Minister, Lewis Corbin. p 48

6 September 1807. Smith GRIGSBY and Nancy Withers. Minister, William Mason, Baptist. p 13

13 May 1787. Loury GRIMES and Jane Settle. Minister, John Pickett, Baptist. p 47

16 January 1800. Daniel GRIMSLEY and Frances Estes. Minister, James Garnett, Baptist. p 10

21 January 1807. William GRIMSLEY and Agge Norman. Minister, Lewis Conner, Baptist. p 19

27 April 1814. John GROVES and Elizabeth Gaunt. Minister, Lewis Conner, Baptist. p 49

-   -   1809. Nathaniel GRUBB and Phebe Bryan. Minister, Abraham Kersey. p 12

31 May 1802. Daniel GRUBBS and Polly Brandon. Minister, Frederick Kabler. p 8

28 June 1801. Enoch GRUBBS and Lucy Dunnaway. Minister, James Garnett, Baptist. p 10

2 January 1806. Abiah GUINN and Elizabeth Curtis. Minister, William Mason, Baptist. p 16

26 December 1781. Enoch GULLEY and Frankey Franklin. Minister, George Eve, Baptist. p 47

8 April 1782. Richard GULLEY and Mary Terry. Minister, George Eve,
Baptist. p 47

24 November 1791. Stephen GUPTON and Phoebe Baxter. Minister, William
Mason, Baptist. p 46

5 January 1791. Frederick HAAGERT and Mary Davis. Minister, William
Carpenter, Lutheran. p 53

23 December 1799. Walter HACKLEY and Chloe Clark. Minister, Reuben
Finnel. p 54

26 June 1798. Carlisle HAINES and Dorcus Williams. Minister, James
Garnett, Baptist. p 54

6 March 1787. John HALEY and Rachel Fleshman. Minister, George Eve,
Baptist. p 51

26 December 1813. James HALL and Jane Willey. Minister, Lewis Conner,
Baptist. p 55

6 July 1803. Thomas HALL and Amy Nalle. Minister, William Mason,
Baptist. p 9

28 January 1790. Reuben HAM and Elizabeth Pembleton. Minister, George
Eve, Baptist. p 54

8 April 1782. Stephen HAM and Rhode Coffer. Minister, George Eve,
Baptist. p 51

1 April 1810. John HAMBRICK and Elizabeth Spencer. Minister, Lewis
Conner. p 55

15 June 1797. Archibald HAMILTON and Maria Shackleford. Minister, Rev.
John Woodville, Rector of St. Mark's Parish, Episcopal Church. St.
Mark's Parish Register.

30 July 1805. William HAMILTON and Sarah Hume. Minister, Frederick
Kabler. p 21

21 December 1800. George HANNARD (?) and Frances Yates. Minister,
James Garnett, Baptist. p 10

27 September 1789. Moses HARBINSON and Ann Barler. Minister, William
Mason, Baptist. p 52

30 October 1792. Martin HARDEN and Jane Aynes. Minister, William
Mason, Baptist. p 53

3 May 1808. Robert HARDIN and Elizabeth Oder. Minister, William Mason,
Baptist. p 13

9 August 1788. Jacob HARDMAN and Nancy Collins. Minister, William Mason, Baptist. p 52

12 September 1802. William HARDEN and Elizabeth Doggett. Minister, Frederick Kabler. p 54

30 January 1784. James HARDY and Polly Balance. Minister, William Mason, Baptist. Green's Notes on Culpeper say Patty. p 52

19 April 1792. John HARFORD and Patty Pinnell. Minister, William Wright. p 50

18 February 1811. John HARMOND and Mary Haney. Minister, Absolem Kinsey. p 20

26 December 1811. Joseph HARPER and Eliza Ann Greenway. Minister, Lewis Conner, Baptist. p 55

16 February 1793. William HARPER and Anna Pulman. Minister, John Pickett, Baptist. p 50

18 December 1788. James HARRIS and Mary Brady. Minister, William Mason, Baptist. p 52

25 January 1787. Jesse HARRIS and Molly Clatterbuck. Minister, Thomas Ammon, Baptist. p 51

14 July 1784. George HARRISON and Nancy Duff. Minister, George Eve, Baptist. p 51

4 April 1793. Obed HARRISON and Frances Lewis. Minister, William Mason, Baptist. p 53

23 December 1786. George HARROLD and Nancy Horsley. Minister, Isham Tatum. p 50

15 December 1785. Elijah HARVEY and Mary Jarrell. Minister, George Eve, Baptist. p 51

30 August 1796. - HAWKINS and Priscilla Freeman. Married at Robert Freeman's. Minister, Rev. John Woodville, Rector of St. Mark's Parish, Episcopal Church. Priscilla, dau. of Robert Freeman, will 31 July 1811; pro. 16 September 1811. St. Mark's Parish Register.

13 January 1807. Archelas HAWKINS and Sealy Yowell. Minister, Lewis Conner, Baptist. p 19

4 June 1795. Dr. Aylett HAWES and Frances Thornton. Married at Col. William Thornton's. Minister, Rev. John Woodville, Rector of St. Mark's Parish, Episcopal Church. St. Mark's Parish Register.

26 April 1805. Elijah HAWKINS and Polly Kilby. Minister, Lewis Conner, Baptist. Green's Notes on Culpeper say Kelly. p 18

26 December 1797. James HAWKINS and Sarah Jones. Minister, William Mason, Baptist. p 52

27 December 1787. John HAWKINS and Nancy Jones. Minister, William Mason, Baptist. p 52

24 December 1795. John HAWKINS and Mahala Randolph. Minister, William Mason, Baptist. p 52

- - -. Matthew HAWKINS and Nancy Wilhoit. Minister, George Sims. Nancy, dau. of Michael Wilhoit, will 10 August 1803; pro. 16 July 1804. She is called Ann in the will. p 54

28 July 1785. William HAWKINS and Anne Bohannon Smith. Minister, Nathaniel Sanders, Baptist. p 51

5 December 1786. William HAWKINS and Dolly Gaines. Minister, William Mason, Baptist. p 52

17 September 1783. James J. HAYDON and Catherine Brarinham. Minister, William Mason, Baptist. This name may be Branham: four Branhams in Culpeper tax book. Green's Notes on Culpeper say Branham. p 51

9 November 1801. Ezekiel HAYNES and Anne Hopkins. Minister, Reuben Finnell. p 10

24 April 1793. George HAYNES and Elizabeth Smith. Minister, John Swindler. p 53

16 August 1794. George HAYNES and S. Ann Smith. Minister, Charles Yates. Green's Notes on Culpeper say Anne S. Smith. p 50

13 July 1786. James HAYNES and Sarah Jackson. Minister, Isham Tatum. p 51

16 December 1790. Jasper HAYNES and ELizabeth Roberts. Minister, James Garnett, Baptist. p 50

14 January 1787. Anthony HAYNIE and Sarah Williams. Minister, John Pickett, Baptist. p 51

3 February 1803. John HAYTON and Sarah Calvert. Minister, Reuben Finnell. Sarah Calvert, dau. of John Calvert and his second wife, Helen Bailey. The groom's name is John Heaton. See John Heaton. p 11

15 March 1795. Richard HAZELL and Nancy Neathers. Minister, John Swindler. p 53

19 July 1785. Benjamin HEAD and Milley Long. Minister, Nathaniel Sanders, Baptist. p 51

26 April 1792. William HEAD and Sally Oliver. Minister, James Garnett, Baptist. p 54

3 February 1803. John HEATON and Sarah Calvert. Minister, Reuben Finnell. Sarah b. 1774 d.s.p. dau. John Calvert and his second wife, Hellen Bailey m. 1772. See John Hayton. p 11

22 October 1799. Joseph HEATON and Ann Antrum. Minister, James Garnett, Baptist. p 54

17 January 1813. Patterson HEATON and Polly Bridwell. Minister, William Mason, Baptist. p 54

20 March 1805. William HEATON and Hannah Heaton. Minister, Charles Yates. p 21

20 November 1789. Alexander HENDERSON and Elizabeth Roebuck. Minister, George Eve, Baptist. p 53

1 March 1792. Benson HENRY and Keziah Manuell. Minister, George Eve, Baptist. p 53

23 July 1795. William HENRY and Eleanor Yancy. Minister, William Mason, Baptist. p 52

28 February 1789. Enoch HENSLEY and Jane Nicholson. Minister, John Pickett, Baptist. p 51

28 December 1800. Enoch HENSLEY and Sally Boling. Minister, John Pickett, Baptist. p 54

24 June 1796. Thomas HERFORD and Sarah Heton. Minister, Charles Yates. p 50

28 May 1797. Thomas HERFORD and Sarah Heaton. Minister, Charles Yates. Both dates given. p 53

9 June -. William HERMAN and Sarah Dennis. Minister, Lewis Conner, Baptist. p 55

20 November 1787. Benjamin HERNDON and Susan Chart. Minister, George Eve, Baptist. p 51

18 August 1791. Edward HERNDON and Nancy Rucker. Minister, George Eve, Baptist. p 53

10 December 1791. Elliott HERNDON and Sally Carter, dau. Charles Carter. Elliott, son of William and Mary (Bohannon) Herndon. Minister, William Mason, Baptist. p 50

1 April 1806. Reuben HERNDON and Becky Marshall. Minister, William Mason, Baptist. p 16

3 January 1804. James HERTON and Sally Evans. Minister, Charles Yates. p 9

29 September 1793. Jacob HESSHONG and Charity Dake. Minister, Nathaniel Pinkard. Tax list says Hessong. p 51

15 December 1811. Silas HICKERSON and Polly Tutt. Minister, William Mason, Baptist. p 55

27 April 1814. William HICKERSON and Judith Ball. Minister, Lewis Conner, Baptist. p 55

4 December 1798. Humphrey HILL and Anne Myrtle. Minister, William Mason, Baptist. p 54

29 September 1792. Jeremiah HILL and Judy Allen. Minister, William Mason, Baptist. p 53

17 May 1792. John HILL and Nancy Palmer. Minister, Lewis Colvin. p 53

28 October 1804. John HILL and Mary Vince. Minister, Reuben Finnell. p 12

21 July 1796. Joseph HILL and Rhoda Marshall. Minister, Frederick Kabler. p 53

18 September 1797. Reuben HILL and Fanny Samuel. Minister, John Pickett, Baptist. p 54

26 December 1785. Robert HILL and Nancy Sutton. Minister, Isham Tatum. p 51

28 October 1786. William HILL and Frances Fennell. Minister, William Mason, Baptist. p 52

2 June 1791. William HILL and Sally Ballenger. Minister, William Mason, Baptist. p 50

24 October 1797. William HILL, Jr., and Isabell Passons. Minister, William Mason, Baptist. p 53

15 January 1798. John HILMAN and Dorothy Garrett. Minister, Frederick Kablar. p 29

15 January 1798. John HILMAN and Dorothea Garnett. Minister, Frederick Kabler. Same as above, both marriages given. p 54

24 May 1792. William HINSLEE and Elizabeth Corbin. Minister, John Pickett, Baptist. Tax list says Hensley. Green's Notes on Culpeper say Henslee. p 53

18 January 1786. Samuel HINSLEY and Rosannah Pierce. Minister, John Pickett, Baptist. p 51

24 February 1803. William HISEL and Nancy Woodward. Minister, Frederick Kabler. This name is Hisle in tax list. p 9

25 January 1797. John HISLE and Polly Hisle. Minister, John Swindler. p 53

3 January 1804. Leonard HISLE and Ramey Jasper. Minister, Charles Yates. p 9

17 March 1789. Robert HISLE and Lydia Jenkins. Minister, William Mason, Baptist. p 52

10 April 1809. Strother HISLE and Elizabeth Smith. Minister, Lewis Conner, Baptist. p 55

27 December 1796. William HISLE and Jane Willis. Minister, Lewis Conner, Baptist. p 53

14 August 1781. William HITCHER and Hannah Hurt. Minister, John Stevenson. p 51

22 March 1800. Stephen HOGG and Sarah Williams. Minister, Absalom Kinsey. p 54

30 January 1794. William HOLDWAY and Elizabeth Thornhill. Minister, William Mason, Baptist. p 51

20 March 1788. John HOLLAND and Catherine Coghill. Minister, William Mason, Baptist. p 52

27 September 1796. Thomas S. HOLLOWAY and Elizabeth Moore. Married at Capt. Moore's. Minister, Rev. John Woodville, Rector of St. Mark's Parish, Episcopal Church. St. Mark's Parish Register.

25 April 1806. John HOLMES and Elizabeth Jones. Minister, Isham Tatum. p 12

4 June 1801. Ephraim HOLOWAY (Holloway) and Susanna Garwood. Minister, Frederick Kabler. p 54

8 December 1785. John HOPPER and Sarah Jett. Minister, John Pickett, Baptist. Sarah, dau. of John Jett, will 21 November 1802; pro. 18 April 1808. p 51

1 October 1815. James Y. HORNER and Polly O. Ferguson. Minister, William Mason, Baptist. p 55

9 April 1804. Samuel HORNER and Julia Sanford. Minister, Reuben Finnell. Julia, dau. of John Sanford, will 10 April 1804; pro. 17 July 1809. p 12

10 January 1792. Matthias HOUSE and Susanna Floyd. Minister, William Carpenter, Lutheran. p 52

8 December 1789. Michael HOUSE and Susanna Zimerman. Minister, William Carpenter, Lutheran. p 53

25 August 1801. John HOWDESHELD and Sarah Harris. Minister, James Garnett, Baptist. Could this name be Houdeshell or Howdeshell? Howdischeld in tax list. p 10

12 April 1790. Thomas HOWELL and Margaret White. Minister, William Carpenter, Lutheran. p 53

12 December 1803. Joseph HUANS and Roda Richards. Minister, Frederick Kabler. p 8

27 December 1792. Armistead HUBBARD and Behethelen Strother. Minister, William Mason, Baptist. p 53

5 June 1797. Taliaferro HUBBARD and Abby Gibson. Minister, Nathaniel Sanders, Baptist. p 52

29 October 1794. Thomas HUBBARD and Sally Strother. Minister, William Mason, Baptist. p 52

28 November 1788. Thomas HUCKERAFT and Nelly Harrison. Minister, William Mason, Baptist. p 52

11 November 1800. Abner HUDSON and Betsy Mason. Minister, William Mason, Baptist. p 54

25 December 1804. Alexander HUDSON and Polly Jones. Minister, Absalom Kinsey. p 10

1 April 1800. Ezekiel HUDSON and Polly Mason. Minister, James Garnett, Baptist. p 54

24 December 1809. Joel HUDSON and Fanny Yager. Minister, James Garnett, Baptist. p 15

9 January 1799. John HUDSON and Jane Appleby. Minister, James Garnett, Baptist. p 54

26 April 1783. Joshua HUDSON and Agnes Brown. Minister, Nathaniel Sanders, Baptist. p 51

27 August 1794. Martin HUDSON and Cynthia Newton. Minister, William Mason, Baptist. p 52

15 October 1789. Moses HUDSON and Mary Clark. Minister, Isham Tatum. p 54

9 May 1798. Reuben HUDSON and Polly Garnett. Minister, William Mason, Baptist. p 52

21 May 1810. Walter HUDSON and Elizabeth Mason. Minister, William Mason, Baptist. p 15

15 January 1801. William HUDSON and Elizabeth Chick. Minister, William Mason, Baptist. p 54

18 December 1799. Henry HUFFMAN and Lucy Read. Minister, John Hickerson, Baptist. p 54

2 February 1795. James HUFFMAN and Letty Arnold. Minister, John Hickerson, Baptist. p 53

8 January 1794. John HUFFMAN and Elizabeth Huffman. Minister, John Hickerson, Baptist. p 54

26 November 1793. Jonas HUFFMAN and Rosanna Deale. Minister, William Carpenter, Lutheran. p 50

19 July 1791. Joseph HUFFMAN and Frances Paine. Minister, John Pickett, Baptist. p 53

22 March 1791. Michael HUFFMAN and Elizabeth Hufman. Minister, William Carpenter, Lutheran. p 53

8 April -. Robert HUFFMAN and Elizabeth Bruce. Minister, John Hickerson, Baptist. p 53

19 January 1790. Daniel HUFMAN and Margaret Bungard. Minister, William Carpenter, Lutheran. p 53

4 December 1787. Ephraim HUFMAN and Mary Ward. Minister, William Mason, Baptist. p 52

16 March 1786. Jacob HUFMAN and Mary Floyd. Minister, William Mason, Baptist. p 52

22 August 1792. Nathaniel HUFMAN and Mary Stomsifer. Minister, William Carpenter, Lutheran. p 52

15 February 1787. Reuben HUFMAN and Caty Hufman. Minister, William Mason, Baptist. p 52

11 March 1792. Samuel HUFMAN and Eve Hufman. Minister, William Carpenter, Lutheran. p 52

23 February 1799. Anthony HUGHES and Elizabeth Adams. Minister, Charles Yates. p 51

11 March 1799. Anthony HUGHES and Elizabeth Adams. Minister, Charles Yates. Both dates given; spelled Hughs in tax list. p 53

15 October 1785. John HUGHES and Ann Waggoner. Minister, John Price, Baptist. p 51

23 March 1798. John HUGHES and Elizabeth Brown. Minister, William Mason, Baptist. p 54

9 December 1794. Robert HUGHES and Elizabeth Strother. Minister, Charles Yates. p 50

7 March 1786. James HUGHES and Betty Putman. Minister, William Mason, Baptist. p 52

25 December 1798. Armistead HUME and Priscilla Colvin. Minister, William Mason, Baptist. p 54

18 October 1785. Charles HUME and Lizy (Lizzie) Banks. Minister, George Eve, Baptist. p 51

18 September 1800. Humphrey HUME and Peggy Lawan. Minister, Frederick Kabler. p 54

18 August 1784. James HUME and Elizabeth Powell. Minister, George Eve, Baptist. p 51

5 January 1792. John HUME and Anna Crigler. Minister, William Carpenter, Lutheran. p 52

29 October 1782. William HUME and Sarah Baker. Minister, George Eve, Baptist. p 50

5 October 1797. James HUMES and Caty Barnes. Minister, William Mason, Baptist. p 53

27 August 1791. Jessee HUMPHRES and Elizabeth Biffy. Minister, John Coons, Baptist. Spelled Humphrey in tax list. p 50

1 January 1787. George HUMPHREY and Polly Lawler. Minister, John Pickett, Baptist. p 51

19 January 1797. Thomas HUMPHREYS and Elizabeth Richards. Minister, Rev. John Woodville, Rector of St. Mark's Parish, Episcopal Church. St. Mark's Parish Register.

16 February 1805. William HUMPHREYS and Milly Carder. Minister, Reuben Finnell. p 14

10 February 1791. Julius HUNT and Mary Brown. Minister, James Garnett, Baptist. p 50

20 December 1803. Robert HUTSON and Elizabeth Jones. Minister, William Mason, Baptist. p 9

9 January 1796. John HYSLE and Frances Pulliam. Minister, William Mason, Baptist. Spelled Hisle in tax list. p 52

9 January 1796. Robert HYSLE and Elizabeth Pulliam. Minister, William Mason, Baptist. p 52

15 July 1802. William INGRAM and Susanna Lawler. Minister, Reubin Finnell. p 11

12 January 1797. Daniel INSKEEP and Rachel Pusy (Pusey). Minister, William Mason, Baptist. p 58

31 January 1797. James INSKEEP, Jr., and Delilah Delanie. Minister, William Mason, Baptist. Green's Notes on Culpeper say Dulaney. p 58

21 December 1801. Job INSKEEP and Patience Bishop. Minister, Frederick Kabler. p 59

24 December 1804. John INSKEEP and Esther Garwood. Minister, Charles Yates. p 21

3 April 1806. Thomas JACOBS and Elizabeth Burgess. Minister, Lewis Conner, Baptist. p 18

18 October 1790. Henry JACKSON and Anna Jones. Minister, James Garnett, Baptist. p 59

23 February 1815. John JACKSON and Sally Sims. Minister, Lewis Conner, Baptist. Green's Notes on Culpeper say Simms. p 60

1 December 1808. William JACKSON and Sarah Houghton. Minister, Reuben Finnell. p 15

2 June 1789. Daniel JAMES and Nancy Graves. Minister, William Mason, Baptist. p 58

21 April 1808. John D. JAMES and Peggy F. Brown. Minister, Lewis Conner, Baptist. p 20

21 February 1783. Samuel JAMES and Frances Bates. Minister, George Eve, Baptist. p 58

6 March 1788. Jeremiah JARRELL and Sarah Sims. Minister, George Eve, Baptist. Green's Notes on Culpeper say Simms. p 58

25 October 1787. William JARRELL and Elizaan Jarrell. Minister, George Eve, Baptist. p 58

26 February 1807. Daniel JASPER and Milly Cheek. Minister, Lewis Conner, Baptist. p 19

16 February 1792. Richard JEE and Mary Remine. Minister, William Wright. p 58

23 December 1794. Alexander JEFFRIES and Frances Favor (Faver). Minister, William Mason, Baptist. p 58

20 March 1800. John JEFFRIES and Rosamond Favor (Faver). Minister, William Mason, Baptist. p 59

21 October 1796. Richard JEFFERIES and Ann C. Pollard. Married at Mrs. Watkins. Minister, Rev. John Woodville, Rector of St. Mark's Parish Episcopal Church. St. Mark's Parish Register.

2 November 1797. Thomas JEFFRIES and Thiza Kegg or Key. Minister, William Mason, Baptist. Green's Notes on Culpeper say Kegg. p 58

8 January 1789. Abraham JENKINS and Nancy Weekly. Minister, William Mason, Baptist. p 58

5 March 1809. Ambrose JENKINS and Susanna Weakley. Minister, Lewis Conner, Baptist. p 60

1 December 1812. Anthony JENKINS and Milly Sisk. Minister, Lewis Conner, Baptist. p 60

17 March 1789. Daniel JENKINS and Agatha Jenkins. Minister, William Mason, Baptist. p 58

19 November 1893. Daniel JENKINS and Sarah Jenkins. Minister, John Swindler. p 59

17 January 1800. Daniel JENKINS and Sarah Jenkins. Minister, Lewis Conner, Baptist. p 59

3 March 1794. Elijah JENKINS and Delilah Jenkins. Minister, William Mason, Baptist. p 58

24 September 1814. Hedgeman JENKINS and Nancy Hensley. Minister, Lewis Conner, Baptist. p 60

6 March 1808. Irvine JENKINS and Peggy Jenkins. Minister, Lewis Conner, Baptist. p 20

10 January 1791. Jeremiah JENKINS and Anne McKensey. Minister, William Mason, Baptist. p 59

16 December 1789. John JENKINS and Elizabeth Story. Minister, William Mason, Baptist. p 59

15 August 1793. Nathan JENKINS and Betsy Weakly. Minister, John Swindler. p 58

7 January 1793. Philip JENKINS and Rebecca Jenkins. Minister, William Mason, Baptist. p 58

29 January 1801. Reubin JENKINS and Lucy Dodson. Minister, Lewis Conner, Baptist. p 59

2 September 1793. Richard JENKINS and Jemima Holoway. Minister, John Swindler. p 57

1 February 1810. Roland JENKINS and Nancy Robbins. Minister, Lewis Conner, Baptist. p 60

15 August 1815. Roley (Roland?) JENKINS and Milly Jenkins. Minister, Lewis Conner, Baptist. p 60

6 February 1801. Silas JENKINS and Caty Nowlin. Minister, James Garnett, Baptist. p 10

6 December 1794. Timothy JENKINS and Elizabeth Smith. Minister, William Mason, Baptist. p 58

16 May 1797. Timothy JENKINS and Nancy Weakley. Minister, Lewis Conner, Baptist. p 59

24 December 1805. Zachariah JENKINS and Ellen Jenkins. Minister, Lewis Conner, Baptist. p 18

25 January 1801. John JENNINGS and Fanny Hunt. Minister, James Garnett, Baptist. p 10

28 January 1797. Amos JENNY and Barbary Gregory. Minister, Frederick Kabler. Green's Notes on Culpeper say Barbara. p 59

27 July 1792. John JESSE and Susanna Carpenter. Minister, William Mason, Baptist. p 58

15 March 1798. Daniel JETT and Lucinda Jones. Minister, Reuben Finnell. p 58

20 May 1815. Francis JETT and Elizabeth Wood. Minister, James Withers, Baptist. p 60

24 December 1804. Jesse JETT and Nancy Chandler. Minister, John Kabler. p 21

8 April 1813. Cleton JOHNSON and Polly Miller. Minister, Lewis Conner, Baptist. p 60

8 June 1793. Allen JOHNSTON and Liney Duncan. Minister, John Pickett, Baptist. Liney, dau. of James Duncan will 17 August 1801; estate divided August 1819. p 57

22 April 1802. Joseph JOHNSTON and Susanna Reed. Minister, Reuben Finnell. p 12

25 February 1806. William JOHNSTON and Mary Ann Yancy. Minister, William Mason, Baptist. p 16

22 March 1787. James JOLLETT and Nancy Walker. Minister, George Eve, Baptist. p 58

25 June 1784. Ambrose JONES and Mary Waggoner. Minister, George Eve, Baptist. p 58

15 February 1790. Baily JONES and Lucy Corbin. Minister, John Pickett, Baptist. p 59

8 April 1815. Charles JONES and Lavinia Glass. Minister, Lewis Conner, Baptist. p 60

31 January 1793. Elijah JONES and Sarah Freeman. Minister, Lewis Corbin. p 59

28 October 1799. Elisha JONES and Elizabeth Freeman. Minister, John Pickett, Baptist. p 59

28 May 1794. Francis JONES and Esther Cowne. Married at Mrs. Watkins by Rev. John Woodville, Rector of St. Mark's Parish, Episcopal Church. p 58

24 December 1800. Gabriel JONES and Patsey Yates. Minister, James Garnett, Baptist. p 10

2 February 1789. Gorden JONES and Siney Browning. Minister, John Pickett, Baptist. p 58

19 March 1792. Henry JONES and Mildred Grigsby. Minister, John Pickett, Baptist. p 59

16 October 1800. James JONES and Nancy Turner. Minister, Frederick Kablar. p 59

27 April 1809/10. James JONES and Rebecca Dyke. Minister, Lewis Conner, Baptist. p 60

2 November 1790. John JONES and Sarah Berry. Minister, William Mason, Baptist. p 59

27 April 1809. John R. JONES and Gilly Marshall. Minister, William Mason, Baptist. p 16

20 July 1813. John JONES and Judy Doggett. Minister, Jesse Butler. p 59

24 August 1813. John JONES and Mary Hisle. Minister, Lewis Conner, Baptist. p 60

21 December 1815. Joseph JONES and Nancy Yates. Minister, Lewis Conner, Baptist. p 60

17 June 1795. Lewis JONES and Nancy Bosts. Minister, John Swindler. p 58

12 February 1789. Moses JONES and Mary Florence. Minister, John Pickett, Baptist. p 58

1 November 1793. Reuben JONES and Dolly Petty. Minister, Isham Tatum. p 59

20 January 1797. Robert JONES and Susanna Bahaughan. Minister, William Mason, Baptist. p 58

5 December 1815. Robert JONES and Sally Crigler. Minister, Lewis Conner, Baptist. p 60

8 November 1797. Standley JONES and Nancy Garnett. Minister, William Mason, Baptist. p 58

22 September 1814. Stephen JONES and Milley Kennard. Minister, William Mason, Baptist. p 60

7 March 1797. Theophilus JONES and Frances Shackelford. Minister, Lewis Corbin. p 59

-   -   -. Thomas JONES and Polly Butler. Minister, Charles Yates. p 59

22 December 1785. Thomas JONES and Agnes Pulliam. Minister, William Mason, Baptist. p 58

23 June 1798. Thomas JONES and Mary Underwood. Minister, Frederick Kablar. p 59

10 January 1799. Timothy JONES and Sarah Cocke. Minister, Frederick Kablar. p 59

23 December 1806. Absolem JORDON and Eliza Eastham. Minister, Lewis Conner, Baptist. p 19

6 July 1791. John JORDAN and Caty Wilson. Minister, John Pickett, Baptist. p 59

6 July 1791. John JORDAN and Catey Willson. Minister, John Pickett, Baptist. Both marriages given. p 57

21 December 1791. Joses JORDAN and Sally Lampkin. Minister, James Garnett, Baptist. p 59

21 March 1791. William JORDAN and Anne Clark. Minister, John Pickett, Baptist. p 59

24 December 1811. George JURY and Damsel Holland. Minister, Lewis Conner, Baptist. p 60

6 June 1811. Reese JURY and Anne Slaughter. Minister, Lewis Conner, Baptist. p 60

28 October 1802. Gabriel KAY and Fanny Waggoner. Minister, William Mason, Baptist. p 62

12 August 1802. James KAY and Sarah Waggoner. Minister, William Mason, Baptist. p 62

3 February 1803. John KAYLOR and Sarah Calvert. b. 1786 d. 1856, dau. George and Lydia Beck (Ralls) Calvert, m. 7 February 1764. (Md. Hist. Mag. Vol. 16 p 198). Original Register. p 18

10 September 1784. Edward KELLY and Barbary Yates. Minister, William Mason, Baptist. Green's Notes on Culpeper say Barbara. p 62

17 February 1803. George KELLY and Jane Field. Minister, Frederick Kabler. p 8

29 October 1790. Jacob KELLY and Peggy Gore. Minister, H. Goodloe. p 62

17 February 1805. James KELLY and Frances Wright. Minister, Isham Tatum. p 21

16 October 1797. John KELLY and Susanna Hill. Minister, John Pickett, Baptist. p 62

6 February 1806. Thomas KELLY and Kesiah Norman. Minister, William
Mason, Baptist. p 16

1 November 1786. William KELLY and Elizabeth Poulter. Minister, William
Mason, Baptist. p 62

27 February 1790. William KELLY and Nancy Terry. Minister, George Eve,
Baptist. p 62

2 February 1789. Benoni KENDRICK and Mary Warner. Minister, John
Pickett, Baptist. p 62

12 January 1805. Jacob KENDRICK and Susanna Jett. Minister, Reuben
Finnell. p 12

26 September 1795. Reuben KENDRICK and Effy (Effie) Rich. Minister,
Lewis Corbin. p 62

15 April 1801. Reuben KENNEDY and Ursula Faulconer. Minister, William
Mason, Baptist. p 62

21 January 1807. David KENNARD and Polly Yates. Minister, William
Mason, Baptist. p 62

4 November 1802. Ames KEYS and Hannah Fennell. Minister, Reuben
Finnell. p 11

10 November 1805. William KIDWELL and Susanna Jett. Minister, Reuben
Finnell. p 14

25 September 1794. Armistead KILBY and Sarah Hawkins. Minister,
William Carpenter, Lutheran. p 62

30 October 1801. Joseph KILBY and Celia Jenkins. Minister, Lewis
Conner, Baptist. p 62

4 November 1794. Benjamin KING and Martha Haywood. Minister, Henry
Fry. p 62

22 October 1795. Benjamin KIRTLEY and Patty Barnes. Minister, William
Mason, Baptist. p 62

11 September 1804. Pleasant KIRTLEY and Tomson Barnes. Minister,
Reuben Finnell. Tomson, dau. of Leonard Barnes, will May 1805;
proved 20 August 1810. p 14

13 August 1805. William KIRTLY and Sarah Lewis. Minister, William
Mason, Baptist. p 15

24 August 1792. Ephraim KLUGG and Elizabeth Major. Minister, George
Eve, Baptist. p 62

6 April 1796. John KLUGG and Nancy Nelson Graves. Minister, William Mason, Baptist. p 62

29 April 1800. George KOONTZ and Mary Threlkeld. Minister, Lewis Conner, Baptist. p 62

2 October 1809. Joseph KOONTZ and Judy Snyder. Minister, William Mason, Baptist. p 17

27 November 1788. Aaron LACEY and Elizabeth Reins. Minister, George Eve, Baptist. p 63

19 November 1810. Elias LAKE and Nancy Jenkins. Minister, Absolem King. p 20

14 September 1797. John LAMPKIN and Elizabeth Wiley. Minister, William Williamson. p 64

10 February 1786. Mark LANDRAM and Nancy Tapp. Minister, John Pickett, Baptist. p 63

7 November 1809. Morgan LAMPKIN and Peggy Cannon. Minister, Lewis Conner, Baptist. p 64

6 June 1798. William A. LANE and Elizabeth Green. Minister, Lewis Conner, Baptist. p 64

4 August 1797. William LANDSOWN and Tryphine Settle. Minister, John Pickett, Baptist. p 64

19 April 1798. William LANSDOWN and Lucy Spiller. Minister, John Swindler. p 64

1 March 1796. Henry LATHAM and Polly Lane. Minister, Rev. John Woodville, Rector of St. Mark's Parish, Episcopal Church. Married at Mr. Lane's. St. Mark's Parish Register.

2 January 1792. Philip LATHAM and Dolly Gray. Minister, Nathaniel Sanders, Baptist. p 64

17 December 1805. William LATHAM and Malinda Gaines. Minister, William Mason, Baptist. p 16

4 December 1804. Walter LAWRENCE and Polly Butler. Minister, Reuben Finnell. p 12

11 July 1801. Samuel LEADMAN and Susanna Stokesbury. Minister, Frederick Kabler. p 64

29 December 1791. David LEAR and Lucy Duval. Minister, William Mason, Baptist. p 63

12 December 1787. James LEAR and Nancy Hill. Minister, John Pickett, Baptist. Nancy, dau. of Richard Hill, will dated 12 November 1801. p 63

31 December 1790. Joshua LEATHER and Elizabeth Ferguson. Minister, William Mason, Baptist. p 64

31 January 1797. Robert G. LECKIE and Sally Taliaferro. Minister, Rev. John Woodville, Rector of St. Mark's Parish, Episcopal Church. St. Mark's Parish Register.

10 August 1793. James LEE and Mary Callahan. Minister, William Mason, Baptist. p 63

15 December 1788. William LEE and Molly Burns. Minister, William Mason, Baptist. p 63

24 December 1806. Richard LEEK and Clara Jenkins. Minister, Lewis Conner, Baptist. p 19

15 February 1788. Robert LEVEL and Elizabeth Harden. Minister, William Mason, Baptist. p 63

10 December 1793. Archelous LEWIS and Jemima Norman. Minister, William Mason, Baptist. p 63

19 December 1815. Benjamin LEWIS and Nancy Mitchell. Minister, Daniel James. p 64

20 July 1786. James LEWIS and Jemima Roberts, dau. Capt. Benjamin Roberts. Minister, William Mason, Baptist. p 63

31 March 1796. Thaddeus LEWIS and Elizabeth Garnett. Minister, William Mason, Baptist. p 63

22 December 1815. Thomas B. LEWIS and Catharine A. Gaines. Minister, William Mason, Baptist. p 65

2 November 1792. Zachariah LEWIS and Mary Stanton. Minister, John Swindler. p 64

6 October 1793. Edward LIGHTFOOT and Martha Eldridge. Minister, William Mason, Baptist. p 63

10 July 1794. Robert LIGHTFOOT and Joanna Delany. Minister, Lewis Corbin. Green's Notes on Culpeper say Dulany. p 64

21 July 1810. Absalom LILLARD and Fanny Hisle. Minister, Lewis Conner, Baptist. p 64

3 March 1799. Benjamin LILLARD and Lucy Brown. Minister, Lewis Conner, Baptist. p 64

25 July 1786. John LILLARD and Rachel Garrott. Minister, William Mason, Baptist. p 63

21 December 1802. John LINGRAM and Betsey Waggoner. Minister, William Mason, Baptist. p 64

9 November 1801. Peter LINK and Hannah Calvert. Minister, Reuben Finnell. Hannah b. 1783, dau. George and Lydia Beck (Ralls) Calvert. M. 7 February 1764. p 11

2 March 1789. John LINSEY (Lindsey) and Ruth Bryan. Minister, John Koonts, Baptist. p 63

26 January 1787. Jacob LIP and Margaret Zimmerman. Minister, William Mason, Baptist. p 63

27 October 1790. John LOCKHEART and Mary Wiley. Minister, Nathaniel Sanders, Baptist. p 64

19 November 1792. Benjamin LONG and Polly Garratt. Minister, Frederick Kablar. p 64

11 January 1787. Bromfield LONG and Lettice Roach. Minister, Nathaniel Sanders, Baptist. p 51

14 October 1805. Gabriel LONG and Lucinda Slaughter. Minister, Lewis Conner, Baptist. Gabriel, son of Reuben Long, will 29 December 1791; pro. 18 June 1792. p 18

30 September 1792. John LONG and Azubah Hawkins. Minister, Nathaniel Sanders, Baptist. p 64

21 August 1794. Thomas LONG and Nancy Shipp. Minister, William Mason, Baptist. p 63

29 August 1799. Thomas LONG and Polly Wharton. Minister, Nathaniel Sanders, Baptist. p 64

3 June 1797. William LONG and Mary Faulconer. Minister, Nathaniel Sanders, Baptist. p 64

28 July 1815. John LOVELL and Frances Beckham. Minister, William Mason, Baptist. p 65

15 March 1799. William LOWERY and Ann Colly. Minister, Charles Yates. p 64

1 August 1784. Francis LOWIN and Lucy Brown. Minister, John Price, Baptist. p 63

4 November 1796. Daniel LOWRY and Mary Cox. Minister, John Swindler. p 64

25 March 1799. William LOWRY and Ann Colley. Minister, Charles Yates. p 63

18 December 1810. John LUCAS and Polly Brown. Minister, William Mason, Baptist. p 15

1 December 1785. Thomas LUCAS and Fanny Wilhoit. Minister, William Mason, Baptist. Fanny, dau. Michael Wilhoit, will 10 August 1803; pro. 16 July 1804. She is called Frances in the will. p 63

12 December 1815. William LUCAS and Ann Moore. Minister, William Mason, Baptist. p 65

9 August 1814. John MAC MANN and Nancy Johnson. Minister, Lewis Conner, Baptist. p 68

2 January 1798. William MC BEE and Sarah McDugley. Minister, Reuben Finnell. p 67

12 January 1792. Daniel MC CARTY and Sally Wharton. Minister, William Wright. p 66

15 December 1792. James MC DANIEL and Anne King. Minister, Henry Fry. p 66

29 June 1791. George MC DONALD and Margaret Dayland. Minister, Isham Tatum. p 66

23 December 1785. John MC DONALD and Frances Putman. Minister, William Mason, Baptist. p 66

8 September 1791. Matthias MC DONALD and Eleanor Jarrell. Minister, George Eve, Baptist. p 67

27 May 1798. Osborn MC DONALD and Elizabeth Murfey (Murphy). Minister, John Hickerson, Baptist. p 67

19 July 1794. William MC DONALD and Mary Darnold. Minister, John Hickerson, Baptist. p 67

15 January 1798. James MC FARLEN and Nancy Wise. Minister, William Mason, Baptist. p 67

7 January 1799. Nathaniel MC GRUDER and Jemimiah Sutherland. Minister, John Pickett, Baptist. Green's Notes on Culpeper say Magruder. p 68

2 January 1800. William MC KAY and Nancy Turner. Minister, Isham Tatum. p 68

31 July 1810. James MC KEBBIN and Anne Read Taylor. Minister, Lewis Conner, Baptist. p 68

6 December 1798. Robert MC KEBBEN and Fanny Boswell. Minister, Lewis Conner, Baptist. p 68

18 March 1808. Strother MC QUEEN and Lucy Yates. Minister, Lewis Conner, Baptist. p 20

9 September 1794. Alexander MC RAE and Harriet Voss. Married at Mr. Edward Voss' by Rev. John Woodville, Rector of St. Mark's Parish, Episcopal Church. p 67

11 February 1799. John MAAR and Elizabeth Whiteley. Minister, Reuben Finnell. p 67

26 March 1787. Jacob MAGGERT and Mary Hufman. Minister, William Mason, Baptist. p 66

2 July 1787. John MAJOR and Ursie Sleett. Minister, William Mason, Baptist. p 66

13 August 1795. William MAJOR and Elizabeth Corbin. Minister, Lewis Corbin. p 67

9 January 1789. John MARGRAVE and Abigail Moore. Minister, William Mason, Baptist. p 66

1 January 1804. James L. MARKHAM and Betsey Porter. Minister, Charles Yates. p 9

16 June 1807. John W. MARSHALL and Palema Moore. Minister, William Mason, Baptist. p 13

3 September 1813. Robert MARSHALL and Mary Dobs (Dobbs). Minister, James Garnett, Baptist. p 68

27 March 1805. Thomas MARSHALL and Mary Bishop. Minister, Reuben Finnell. p 14

30 July 1806. Thomas MARSHALL and Matilda Wallace. Minister, William Mason, Baptist. Index says Malenda. p 16

11 July 1788. John MARSTEN and Rachel Spicer. Minister, William Mason, Baptist. p 66

2 November 1788. John MARTIN and Nelly Nicholson. Minister, William Mason, Baptist. p 66

5 January 1791. John MARTIN and Mary Long. Minister, William Mason, Baptist. p 67

23 October 1796. William MARTIN and Lucy Sanford. Minister, Frederick Kabler. p 67

12 June 1806. Willis MARTIN and Agatha Gaunt. Minister, William Mason, Baptist. p 16

14 July 1805. Elijah MASON and Ann Wood. Minister, Reuben Finnell. p 14

23 December 1806. Enoch MASON and Fanny Ramey. Minister, William Mason, Baptist. p 13

25 December 1793. James MASON and Susanna Tapp. Minister, John Hickerson, Baptist. p 67

12 December 1791. Joel MASON and Sally Brown. Minister, William Mason, Baptist. p 66

24 September 1806. Nelson MASON and Mary Newton. Minister, Lewis Conner, Baptist. p 19

11 October 1815. Silas MASON and Patsey Garnett. Minister, William Mason, Baptist. p 69

12 August 1802. John MATHENY and Betsy Smith. Minister, Frederick Kabler. p 8

7 October 1794. James MATHEWS and Sally Steward. Minister, John Hickerson, Baptist. p 67

- - 1809. Joseph MATLOCK and Matilda Cornett. Minister, Abraham Kersey. p 12

1 February 1810. Abraham MAURY and Elizabeth Wilhoit. Minister, William Mason, Baptist. p 15

20 October 1803. John MAURY and Frances Long. Minister, William Mason, Baptist. p 9

28 February 1797. Henry MENEFEE and Nancy Hughes. Minister, Lewis Conner, Baptist. p 68

2 January 1811. Henry MENEFEE and Philadelphia Yancey. Minister, Lewis Conner, Baptist. p 68

4 January 1815. Jared MENEFEE and Fanny Hopkins. Minister, Lewis Conner, Baptist. p 68

27 January 1814. John MENEFEE and Sally Brown. Minister, Lewis Conner, Baptist. p 68

24 March 1808. Jonas MENIFEE and Polly Yancy. Minister, Lewis Conner, Baptist. p 20

20 December 1795. John MENEFEE and Elizabeth Huse. Minister, Charles Yates. p 66

27 October 1808. John MENEFEE and Lucy Partlow. Minister, Lewis Conner, Baptist. p 20

16 March 1797. Larkin MENEFEE and Lucy Yancy. Minister, William Mason, Baptist. p 67

15 April 1806. Robert MENEFEE and Polly Waggoner. Minister, Reuben Finnell. p 14

13 December 1790. William MENEFEE and Mary Strother. Minister, John Hickerson, Baptist. p 67

28 March 1811. William MENEFEE and Catharine Partlow. Minister, Lewis Conner, Baptist. p 68

25 April 1799. Benjamin MERSHON and Anne Jett. Minister, John Hickerson, Baptist. p 68

29 January 1814. James MIDDLETON and Lucy Jenkins. Minister, Lewis Conner, Baptist. p 68

11 November 1790. Adam MILLER and Polly Wilhoit. Minister, Lewis Conner, Baptist. p 67

9 January 1800. John MILLER and Alice Wright. Minister, Reuben Finnell. p 67

12 March 1793. Michal MILLER and Rebecca Carpenter. Minister, William Carpenter, Lutheran. p 67

12 January 1815. Samuel MILLER and Delena Bywaters. Minister, Lewis Conner, Baptist. p 68

12 April 1794. Wollery MING or MENG and Esther Morris. Minister, William Mason, Baptist.

2 January 1794. Waller MINOR and Mary Cowin. Minister, William Mason, Baptist. p 66

3 December 1792. Benjamin MITCHELL and Caty Garnett. Minister, William Mason, Baptist. p 66

6 January 1790. Fisher MITCHELL and Molly Gosney. Minister, James Garnett, Baptist. p 67

23 April 1801. John MITCHELL, Jr., and Jannet Newton. Minister, William Mason, Baptist. p 68

13 January 1803. John A. MITCHELL and Catharine Hanson. Minister, Reuben Finnell. p 11

26 March 1787. Mark MITCHELL and Mary Rider. Minister, William Mason, Baptist. p 66

22 February 1793. Thomas MITCHELL and Peggy Chambers. Minister, Nathaniel Sanders, Baptist. p 67

3 December 1793. William MITCHELL and Lucy Garnett. Minister, William Mason, Baptist. p 66

17 January 1787. Willis MITCHELL and Sarah Mitchell. Minister, Nathaniel Sanders, Baptist. p 66

29 November 1793. James MOBLEY and Elizabeth Herrin. Minister, William Mason, Baptist. p 66

16 June 1785. George MONDAY and Isabel Myrtle. Minister, William Mason, Baptist. p 66

31 August 1797. Roger MOODIE and Anne - . p 67

16 October 1781. William MOONY and Sarah Walker. Minister, George Eve, Baptist. p 66

13 September 1786. Abraham MOOR and Elizabeth Cinne. Minister, William Mason, Baptist. p 66

7 February 1788. Elnathan MOOR and Polly Scott. Minister, William Mason, Baptist. p 66

29 August 1799. Anthony MOORE and Jane Adams. Minister, Reuben Finnell. p 67

20 December 1813. David MOORE and Hannah Woodard. Minister, Lewis Conner, Baptist. p 68

12 January 1793. Harbin MOORE and Ann Tutt. Minister, William Mason, Baptist. p 67

3 November 1809. Thomas MOORE and Polly Hughes. Minister, Lewis Conner, Baptist. p 68

11 August 1796. Timothy MOORE and Mary Gully. Minister, William Mason, Baptist. p 66

26 December 1799. William MOREHEAD and Polly Triplett. Minister, William Mason, Baptist. p 67

12 March 1804. Walter MORELAND and Rachel Duke. Minister, Reuben Finnell. Old index says Dahe. p 12

23 January 1800. Daniel MORGAN and Sarah Thomas. Minister, Charles Yates. p 68

1 December 1801. Edmond MORRIS and Sally Reynolds Partlow. Minister, William Mason, Baptist. p 68

25 October 1795. Thomas MORRIS and Sally Kinnard. Minister, Lewis Conner, Baptist. p 67

11 March 1808. Caleb MORRISON and Sally Browning. Minister, Reuben Finnell. p 15

4 November 1797. John MORRISON and Histher Douglas. Minister, John Pickett, Baptist. p 68

26 December 1797. Elijah MOSS and Susanna Earrol. Minister, William Williamson. p 67

24 August 1809. Elisha MOSS and Mary Groves. Minister, Lewis Conner, Baptist. p 68

11 March 1788. William MOTHERSHEAD and Lucy Long. Minister, Nathaniel Sanders, Baptist. p 66

2 December 1795. Benjamin MOZINGO and Mary Little. Minister, John Swindler. p 67

10 March 1811. William L. MUNDY and Anna Porter. Minister, Lewis Conner, Baptist. p 68

11 May 1803. Dennis MURPHY and Sally Marshall. Minister, Frederick Kabler. p 8

24 December 1805. John MURPHY and Sally Sedwick. Minister, Reuben Finnell. p 14

30 November 1786. Martin MURPHY and Sarah Glass. Minister, John Pickett, Baptist. p 66

10 March 1810. Thomas MURPHY and Elizabeth Edrington. Minister, Frederick Kabler. p 68

6 December 1808. Jacob MYERS and Maria Calvert. Minister, Lewis Conner, Baptist. Maria b. 1791, dau. of George and Lydia Beck (Ralls) Calvert, M. 7 February 1764. (Md. Hist. Mag. Vol. 16 p 197). p 20

16 January 1787. Benjamin MYRTLE and Frances Broyle. Minister, William Mason, Baptist. p 66

26 April 1792. James NALLE and Peggy Parks. Minister, William Mason, Baptist. Peggy, dau. Richard Parks, Will 2 March 1817; pro. 18 August 1817. p 70

29 September 1785. John NALLE and Lucy Hill. Minister, William Mason, Baptist. Lucy, dau. William Hill, will 25 January 1809; pro. 20 April 1812. p 70

5 November 1793. Larkin NASH and Elizabeth Hanye. Minister, John Hickerson, Baptist. p 70

15 April 1802. John NETHERS and Esther Dyke. Minister, Lewis Conner, Baptist. p 71

11 July 1789. Andrew NEWMAN and Mary Ann Fennell. Minister, William Mason, Baptist. p 70

10 September 1790. George NEWMAN and Polly Born. Minister, Isham Tatum. p 70

22 December 1789. James NEWMAN and Mary Early. Minister, George Eve, Baptist. p 70

5 February 1789. Robert NEWMAN and Elizabeth Latham. Minister, William Mason, Baptist. p 70

20 December 1804. William H. NEWMAN and Jemimah Tucker. Minister, Reuben Finnell. p 14

21 December 1803. Benjamin NEWLIN and Nancy Kirtly. Minister, William Mason, Baptist. p 9

7 March 1801. Michel NICHOLS and Sally Miller. Minister, James Garnett, Baptist. p 10

16 October 1786. William NICHOLS and Frances Randolph. Minister, William Mason, Baptist. p 70

4 December 1792. Benjamin NICHOLSON and Elizabeth Shackelford. Minister, Lewis Corbin. p 70

24 October 1790. John NICHOLSON and Phoebe Jenkins. Minister, William Mason, Baptist. p 70

17 July 1793. James NICKENS and Mary Peggy Berden. Minister, John Hickerson, Baptist. p 70

1 January 1802. Joseph NICKLIN and Elizabeth Calvert. Minister, Reuben Finnell. Joseph Hicklin b. 1776, d. 1853. Elizabeth, dau. John and Hellen (Bailey) Calvert, b. 1777 d. 1833. Joseph, son of Joseph and Martha (Richards) Nicklin. p 11

21 January 1811. George NICOL and Hester Hains. Minister, Absolem Kinsey. p 20

23 April 1810. Hezekiah NOLLEY and Susanna Bourn. Minister, Absolem King. p 20

23 December 1803. Zephiniah NOOE (Noe) and Sarah Kirtley. Minister, Frederick Kabler. p 10

12 September 1793. Courtney NORMAN and Alice Jett. Minister, William Mason, Baptist. p 70

19 December 1799. Isaac NORMAN and Sally Watts. Minister, Frederick Kabler. p 70

2 February 1806. Joseph NORMAN and Mary Davis. Minister, Isham Tatum. p 12

20 April 1796. Thomas NORMAN and Sally Utterback. Minister, Lewis Corbin. p 70

1 June 1797. Manyard OAKS and Sukey Rosson. Minister, William Mason, Baptist. p 71

22 December 1795. Joel ODAR and Jane Fletcher. Minister, John Woodville, Rector of St. Mark's Parish, Episcopal Church. Married at Mrs. Vernon's. p 71

29 March 1804. Jeremiah ODELL and Polly Menefee. Minister, Lewis Conner, Baptist. p 17

31 October 1805. Gabriel ODER and Maria Monroe. Minister, Lewis Conner, Baptist. p 18

9 December 1807. John ODER and Nancy Jenkins. Minister, Lewis Conner, Baptist. p 19

13 January 1803. John OLDE and Nancy Yates. Minister, Frederick Kabler. p 9

6 August 1807. Barnett O'NEAL and Sally Embry. Minister, Lewis Conner, Baptist. p 19

18 September 1808. John O'NEAL and Elizabeth Embry. Minister, Lewis Conner, Baptist. p 20

8 April 1794. John ONEALE and Juda Suttle. Minister, John Swindler. p 71

10 February 1789. John ONEALS and Phoebe Scott. Minister, George Eve, Baptist. Oneal in tax list. p 71

15 January 1807. Daniel O'NEEL and Sarah Jennings. Minister, Reuben Finnell. p 14

4 November 1789. William ORR and Polly Gaines. Minister, Isham Tatum. Mary in the will of her father Richard Gaines 4 February 1807; pro. 16 February 1807. p 71

31 January 1788. Obadiah OVERTON and Ellender Crow. Minister, George Eve, Baptist. p 71

20 December 1791. Willis OVERTON and Susanna Sturman. Minister, George Eve, Baptist. p 71

15 August 1805. Harrison OWEN and Lucy Vaughan. Minister, Frederick Kabler. p 21

28 July 1788. Daniel PALMER and Susanna Hensley. Minister, John Pickett, Baptist. p 72

17 August 1797. John PARRY and Susanna Utterback. Minister, William Williamson. p 73

12 January 1796. Richard PARKS and Ann Faver. Minister, Nathaniel Pinckard. p 73

22 December 1808. Elisha PARTLOW and Frances Menefee. Minister, Lewis Conner, Baptist. p 73

24 March 1789. James PASSONS and Lucy Myrtle. Minister, William Mason, Baptist. p 72

28 May 1804. Thomas PATTON and Betsey Moss. Minister, Reuben Finnell. p 12

25 May 1801. Bennett PAYNE and Polly McKensey. Minister, James Garnett, Baptist. p 10

14 January 1813. Elias PAYNE and Nancy Curtis. Minister, William Mason, Baptist. p 73

17 February 1795. Richard PAYNE and Mary Major. Minister, Rev. John Woodville, Rector of St. Mark's Parish, Episcopal Church. Married at Samuel Major's. Mary, dau. of Mary Major, will 23 August 1809, pro. 18 September 1809. p 72

8 January 1793. William PAYNE and Avee Garnett. Minister, Isham Tatum. p 73

4 May 1793. James PEEK and Sharlotte Clatterbuck. Minister, William Mason, Baptist. p 72

10 February 1800. Edmund PENDLETON and Elizabeth Ward. Minister, John Pickett, Baptist. p 73

28 October 1794. Edward PENDLETON and Sarah Strother. Minister, Lewis Corbin. p 73

15 March 1796. Henry PENDLETON and Elizabeth Pendleton. Minister, Rev. John Woodville, Rector of St. Mark's Parish, Episcopal Church. St. Mark's Parish Register.

28 January 1794. Thomas PENDLETON and Jane Farmer. Minister, Jane Hickerson, Baptist. p 73

29 November 1797. John PENNINGTON and Catherine Vint. Minister, Charles Yates. p 73

28 June 1808. Charles PERRY and Ann Washington. Minister, James Garnett, Baptist. p 12

3 April 1810. Pierce PERRY and Ellen Corbin. Minister, William Mason, Baptist. p 15

14 September 1786. Peter PETERS and Mary Sims. Minister, William Mason, Baptist. Green's Notes on Culpeper say Simms. p 72

19 April 1808. Foushee PETTIT and Fanny Vaughan. Minister, Lewis Conner, Baptist. p 20

30 October 1800. Jacob PETTIT and Stalley Fryer. Minister, Lewis Conner, Baptist. p 73

26 September 1805. George PETTY and Patsey Hansbrough. Minister, Frederick Kabler. p 21

19 January 1797. James PETTY and Polly Alsop. Minister, William Mason, Baptist. p 72

23 September 1807. Larkin PETTY and Polly Fore. Minister, William Mason, Baptist. p 13

21 December 1799. Rolly PETTY and Frances Hill. Minister, John Pickett, Baptist. Spelled Rawleigh in tax list. p 73

16 March 1815. Benjamin PEYTON and Henrietta Swindler. Minister, Lewis Conner, Baptist. p 74

15 April 1792. George PEYTON and Susanna Cogill. Minister, John Coons. p 72

10 December 1809. Isaac PEYTON and Nancy Grimsley. Minister, Lewis Conner, Baptist. p 73

31 July 1800. Isaiah PEYTON and Milly Campbell. Minister, Absalom Kinsey. p 73

19 December 1808. James PEYTON and Betsey Sanders. Minister, William Mason, Baptist. p 16

28 November 1805. John PEYTON and Polly Butler. Minister, Reuben Finnell. p 14

25 December 1800. Joseph PEYTON and Nancy Estes. Minister, James Garnett, Baptist. p 10

4 June 1792. Thomas PEYTON and Anne Lampkin. Minister, Nathaniel Sanders, Baptist. p 72

31 October 1808. George PHILLIPS and Elizabeth Harshbarger. Minister, Lewis Conner, Baptist. p 20

25 August 1786. John PHILLIPS and Eleanor Casey. Minister, Isham Tatum. p 72

26 October 1789. Solomon PHILIPS and Hannah Hufman. Minister, John Pickett, Baptist. p 73

22 March 1798. John PICKETT and Polly Samuel. Minister, John Hickerson, Baptist. p 73

31 May 1782. James PIERCE and Elizabeth Croaford (Crafford or Crawford). Minister, George Eve, Baptist. Green's Notes on Culpeper say Crawford. p 72

20 September 1786. John PIERCE and Nancy McQuin. Minister, John Pickett, Baptist. Green's Notes on Culpeper say McGuinn. p 72

22 September 1786. John PIERCE and Sally Jeffries. Minister, John Pickett, Baptist. p 72

23 August 1781. Shadrack PIERSON and Rachel Clinch. Minister, James Stevenson, Rector of St. Mark's Parish, Episcopal Church. Also spelled Pearson. p 72

30 August 1799. Spencer PINCHARD (Pinkard?) and Betsy Marshall. Minister, William Mason, Baptist. p 73

22 December 1791. Thomas PINER and Elizabeth Swindler. Minister, Isham Tatum. p 72

26 November 1799. William R. PINNELL and Anna Murphy. Minister, Reubin Finnell. p 73

21 October 1790. John PITCHER and Lucy Thornhill. Minister, Isham Tatum. p 73

19 June 1793. John PITTS and Priscilla Utterback. Minister, Lewis Corbin. p 73

9 March 1805. Francis POE and Mary Allen. Minister, Reuben Finnell. p 12

24 October 1794. William POE and Susanna Doggett. Minister, Lewis Corbin. p 73

7 December 1797. Elijah POLLARD and Catherine Garner. Minister, William Mason, Baptist. p 72

29 December 1812. James POLLARD and Amelia Tutt. Minister, Lewis Conner, Baptist. p 74

17 September 1798. Robert POMPKINS and Polly Gray. Minister, William Mason, Baptist. p 72

11 December 1795. Gerard POPHAM and Keziah Boughan. Minister, Lewis Conner, Baptist. p 73

2 November 1788. Humphrey POPHAM and Betsy Hawkins. Minister, William Mason, Baptist. Betsy, dau. Mathew Hawkins, will 27 May 1820; pro. 19 June 1820: calls her Betty. p 72

27 December 1795. John POPHAM and Elizabeth Brown. Minister, Lewis Conner, Baptist. p 73

14 June 1792. Reuben PORCH and Nancy Asher. Minister, Nathaniel Sanders, Baptist. p 72

12 January 1791. William PORTER and Ellen Morton. Minister, Isham Tatum. p 73

1 September 1796. William PORTER and Polly McCauley Duncanson at "Clover Hill". Minister, Rev, John Woodville, Rector of St. Mark's Parish, Episcopal Church. St. Mark's Parish Register.

16 December 1788. William POULTER and Jane Willis. Minister, William Mason, Baptist. p 72

25 December 1788. William POULTER, Jr., and Naney Mardes. Minister, William Mason, Baptist. p 72

8 June 1798. Lott POUND and Patsey Faulconer. Minister, Frederick Kabler. p 73

14 August 1810. Ambrose POWELL and Frances Payne. Minister, Daniel James. p 21

16 June 1786. Benjamin POWELL and Elizabeth Green. Minister, Isham Tatum. p 72

28 February 1787. Micajah POWELL and Mary Wilhoit. Minister, Thomas Ammon, Baptist. p 72

23 January 1810. William POWELL and Betsey B. Sims. Minister, William Mason, Baptist. Green's Notes on Culpeper say Simms. p 15

24 February 1813. Jesse PRATT and Milly Johnson. Minister, Lewis Conner, Baptist. p 74

16 December 1789. Josiah PRATT and Mary Beckham. Minister, William Mason, Baptist. p 73

7 January 1796. Thomas PRATT and Elizabeth Smith. Minister, William Mason, Baptist. p 72

14 December 1805. Thomas PRATT and Celia Golden. Minister, William Mason, Baptist. p 16

12 October 1815. George PRITCHETT and Elizabeth Compton. Minister, James Withers, Baptist. p 74

20 November 1793. Samuel PRITCHETT and Rebecca Anderson. Minister, John Swindler. p 73

1 February 1791. William PRITCHETT and Nelly Dodson. Minister, William Mason, Baptist. p 73

2 February 1792. Robert PULLIAM and Dibly Bumgarner. Minister, William Mason, Baptist. p 72

18 January 1786. Thomas PULLIAM and Keziah Brown. Minister, William Mason, Baptist. p 72

19 January 1792. William PURVIS and Jane Burk. Minister, Lewis Corbin. Spelled Purvess in tax list. p 72

25 December 1809. Edward S. QUISENBERRY and Nancy Threlkeld. Minister, Daniel James. p 20

9 September 1803. John RACE and Ellen Williams. Minister, Reuben Finnell. p 11

2 February 1802. Moses RACE and Mary Tomlin. Minister, Reuben Finnell. p 11

25 May 1788. Daniel RAILSBACK and Rosany Clore. Minister, William Mason, Baptist. p 76

8 February 1789. George RAISOR and Frankey Majors. Minister - . p 75

22 December 1803. Jacob RAMEY and Mary Latham. Minister, William Mason, Baptist. p 9

15 August 1798. William RAMSBOTTOM and Clary Jenkins. Minister, Lewis Conner, Baptist. Green's Notes on Culpeper say Clara. p 77

8 December 1790. James RANDOLPH and Susanna Duval. Minister, William Mason, Baptist. p 76

23 December 1793. Jediah RANDOLPH and Nancy Jennings. Minister, William Mason, Baptist. p 75

29 December 1780. Christopher RASSOR and Sarah Sims. Minister, Isham Tatum. Christian Razor in tax list. Green's Notes on Culpeper say Simms. p 75

6 February 1786. Jacob RAXOR and Susanna Snyder. Minister, William Mason, Baptist. Razor in tax list. p 76

26 November 1792. Griffin READ and Elizabeth Chowning. Minister, Lewis Corbin. Green's Notes on Culpeper say Chewning. p 76

1 July 1804. John REASON and Mary Moss. Minister, Reuben Finnell. p 12

21 September 1792. Daniel RECTOR and Elizabeth Coons. Minister, John Hickerson, Baptist. p 76

23 January 1804. Reuben REDMAN and Milly Redman. Minister, Charles Yates. p 9

6 November 1792. Griffin REED and Elizabeth Chowning. Minister, Lewis Colvin. Green's Notes on Culpeper say Chewning. p 76

26 December 1795. Gideon REES and Ann Allen. Minister, Frederick Kabler. Ann, dau. of William Allen, will 12 July 1799; proved 16 September 1799. p 76

23 December 1812. John REVERCOMB and Polly Jenkins. Minister, Lewis Conner, Baptist. p 77

11 January 1786. Edward REYNOLDS and Sary (Sarah) Fewell. Minister, William Mason, Baptist. p 76

16 April 1790. Robert REYNOLDS and Mary Tailiaferro. Minister, William Mason, Baptist. p 76

23 December 1790. Benjamin RICE and Elizabeth Tinsley. Minister, William Carpenter, Lutheran. p 76

29 October 1806. Elijah RICE and Jallah (?) Garnett. Minister, James Garnett, Baptist. p 14

8 December 1808. Ezekiel RICE and Fanny Garnett. Minister, William Mason, Baptist. p 16

24 October 1799. James B. RICE and Susanna Wallis. Minister, William Mason, Baptist. p 77

6 January 1791. John RICE and Lucy Jones. Minister, James Garnett, Baptist. p 75

8 April 1806. Thomas RICHARDS and Nancy Homes. Minister, James Garnett, Baptist. p 15

22 June 1801. John RICHARDSON and Susanna Clatterback. Minister, Lewis Conner, Baptist. p 77

21 September 1815. Thomas RICHARDSON and Polly McCarty. Minister, Lewis Conner, Baptist. p 77

24 December 1801. Jarrard RICKETTS and Elizabeth E. Compton. Minister, Reuben Finnell. p 11

6 December 1787. Archabud (Archabald?) RIDER and Peggy Gaines. Minister, William Mason, Baptist. p 76

23 January 1806. John RIDER and Patsey Lillard. Minister, Lewis Conner, Baptist. p 18

10 December 1785. Jacob RIFFLER and Mildred Burris. Minister, John Pickett, Baptist. p 75

24 August 1815. John ROBERSON and Birley Rakestraw. Minister, William Mason, Baptist. p 77

19 February 1799. George ROBERTS and Ann Hill. Minister, William Mason, Baptist. Ann, dau. of William Hill, will 25 January 1809; pro. 20 April 1812. p 77

21 March 1792. Henry ROBERTS and Elizabeth Maddox. Minister, John Pickett, Baptist. p 76

18 March 1792. James ROBERTS and Betsey Roberts. Minister, Lewis Calvin. p 76

15 January 1801. John ROBERTS and Susanna Abbott. Minister, George Sims. Susanna, dau. of Roger Abbott, will 21 February 1809; proved 17 April 1809. p 77

23 December 1794. William ROBERTSON, Jr., and Ann Grinnan. Minister, Rev. John Woodville, Rector of St. Mark's Parish, Episcopal Church. Married at Mr. Danniel Grinnan's. p 76

17 August 1797. Spencer ROBINSON and Mary Utterback. Minister, William Williamson. p 76

22 December 1811. George RODGERS and Mary Turner. Minister, Daniel James. p 77

13 November 1796. Joseph RODGERS and - Stallard. Minister, John Pickett, Baptist. Rogers in tax list. p 77

20 - 1798. Aaron ROGERS and Elizabeth Bumgarner. Minister, Lewis Conner, Baptist. p 77

15 October 1792. Burgess ROGERS and Sophia Miller. Minister, Isham Tatum. p 75

10 February 1791. John ROGERS and Sarah Kirtly. Minister, George Eve, Baptist. p 77

17 February 1808. John ROLLINS and Mary Monroe. Minister, Lewis Conner, Baptist. p 19

4 July 1787. Moses ROLLINS and Mary Smith. Minister, George Eve, Baptist. p 75

22 March 1815. William ROLLINS and Nancy Golden. Minister, Lewis Conner, Baptist. p 77

25 December 1794. Robert ROMAN and Polly Smith. Minister, William Mason, Baptist. p 76

11 January 1807. John ROSS and Sally Marshall. Minister, James Garnett, Baptist. p 14

25 October 1791. Reuben ROSS and Sally Terrell. Minister, Nathaniel Sanders, Baptist. p 77

28 September 1802. Stevin ROSS and Susanna Bansell. Minister, Frederick Kabler. p 8

20 April 1784. William ROSS and Jane Oneals. Minister, William Mason, Baptist. p 76

19 November 1800. Gabriel ROSSON and Polly Pinkard. Minister, William Mason, Baptist. p 77

9 November 1796. Jesse ROSSON and Ann Smith "at my own house". Minister, Rev. John Woodville, Rector of St. Mark's Parish, Episcopal Church. St. Mark's Parish Register.

26 January 1801. David ROSSAU and Caty Gaines. Minister, Isham Tatum. Caty, dau. Richard Gaines, will 4 February 1807; pro. 16 February 1807. Rosson in Green's Notes on Culpeper p 49. (wills). p 77

20 October 1812. William ROUT and Peggy Mitchell. Minister, James Garnett, Baptist. p 77

11 January 1794. John ROUTT and Sarah Tutt. Minister, William Mason, Baptist. p 75

19 August 1794. John ROUTT, Jr., and Elizabeth Duncan. Minister, William Mason, Baptist. Elizabeth, dau. of James Duncan, will 17 August 1801; estate divided August 1819. p 75

9 January 1791. Benjamin ROWE and Mary Powell. Minister, Isham Tatum. p 77

31 March 1787. William ROWE and Sally Towles. Minister, William Mason, Baptist. p 76

5 September 1787. William RUCH and Nancy Crain. Minister, William Mason, Baptist. p 76

22 October 1782. James RUCKER and Mildred Tinsley. Minister, George Eve, Baptist. p 75

22 September 1791. Joel RUCKER and Amey Young. Minister, George Eve, Baptist. p 76

28 December 1785. Reuben RUCKER and Mary Terrill. Minister, Isham Tatum. p 75

9 October 1806. Robert RUCKER and Sally Gaines. Minister, William Mason, Baptist. Sally, dau. of Richard Gaines, will 4 February 1807; pro. 16 February 1807. p 12

30 October 1795. John RUDISILLEY and Elizabeth Vaughan. Minister, Charles Yates. p 75

13 December 1792. Philip RUDICILLA and Mary Vaughan. Minister, William Mason, Baptist. p 76

10 January 1797. William RUDISILLA and Keziah Baughn. Minister, Lewis Corbin. p 76

4 November 1790. William RUMSEY and Mary Gaines. Minister, William Mason, Baptist. p 76

13 October 1790. Ephraim RUSH and Elizabeth Moore. Minister, William Mason, Baptist. p 76

19 September 1788. John RUSSELL and Jane Reynolds. Minister, William Mason, Baptist. p 76

9 March 1809. William RUTTER and Polly Creal. Minister, Lewis Conner, Baptist. p 77

17 October 1786. Daniel RYNOR and Elizabeth Fleshman. Minister, Isham Tatum. Spelled Ryner in tax list. p 76

9 December 1794. Jonas SAFER and Mary Donaway (Dunaway). Minister, Charles Yates. p 79

26 May 1795. Richard Rice SAILOR and Elizabeth Hall " near Fredericksburg". Minister, Rev. John Woodville, Rector of St. Mark's Parish, Episcopal Church. See Richard Rice Gailor. St. Mark's Parish Register.

4 November 1784. Joseph SAMPSON and Polly Coleman. Minister, William Mason, Baptist. p 80

10 November 1784. William SAMPSON and Sally Coleman. Minister, William Mason, Baptist. p 80

16 October 1788. Moses SAMUEL and Rosanna Zimerman. Minister, -. p 79

23 December 1806. James SANDERS and Elizabeth Camp. Minister, William Mason, Baptist. p 13

3 December 1796. John SANDERS and Sally Williams. Minister, Nathaniel Sanders, Baptist. p 80

26 February 1809. John SANFORD and Amelia Hanes. Minister, Absalom Kinsey. p 17

17 December 1799. Charles SCOGGAN and Lucy Ferguson. Minister, John Pickett, Baptist. p 82

3 August 1786. Moore SCOTT and Rachel Evins Popham. Minister, William Mason, Baptist. p 80

10 March 1789. Reuben SCOTT and Susanna Petty. Minister, Isham Tatum. p 79

25 February 1800. Young SCOTT and Sally Tapp. Minister, John Pickett, Baptist. p 82

13 February 1798. Fielding SEAL and Rebecca West. Minister, William Carpenter, Lutheran. p 83

23 December 1802. Zadoch SEDWICK and Elizabeth Murphy. Minister, Reuben Finnell. p 11

3 January 1807. Benjamin SESSON and Elizabeth Brown. Minister, Reuben Finnell. Old Index says Sisson. p 12

1 November 1804. Abner SETTLE and Nancy Pennell (Finnell?). Minister, Reuben Finnell. p 12

2 April 1808. Abraham SETTLE and Abigail Cummins. Minister, Reuben Finnell. p 15

4 December 1806. Calvert SETTLE and Sally Turner. Minister, Lewis Conner, Baptist. p 19

15 December 1799. James SETTLE and Elizabeth Spilman. Minister, John Hickerson, Baptist. p 82

10 December 1809. Joseph SETTLE and Elizabeth Miller. Minister, Lewis Conner, Baptist. p 83

29 October 1811. Joseph SETTLE and Rachel Jordan. Minister, Lewis Conner, Baptist. p 83

12 September 1786. Marryman SETTLE and Mary Dill. Minister, John Pickett, Baptist. p 79

14 August 1804. William SETTLE and Nancy Pickett. Minister, Reuben Finnell. Nancy, dau. John and Hannah (Withers) Pickett. John Pickett's will 9 July 1803; pro. 17 September 1803. p 14

11 March 1798. Charles SHACKELFORD and Polly Menefee. Minister, Reuben Finnell. p 81

4 March 1784. Dudley SHACKELFORD and Winifred Waterspon. Minister, William Mason, Baptist. Spelled Shackelford in tax list. See Dudley Chackelford.

2 October 1813. James SHACKELFORD and Catharine Basey. Minister, Lewis Conner, Baptist. p 83

2 August 1794. John SHACKELFORD and Peggy Newby. Minister, William Mason, Baptist. p 80

9 June 1808. John SHACKELFORD and Sally Coleman. Minister, William Mason, Baptist. p 13

27 January 1800. Mallory SHACKLEFORD and Nancy McQueen. Minister, Absalom Kinsey. p 83

10 March 1802. Mallory SHACKLEFORD and Mary Coleman. Minister, William Mason, Baptist. p 82

16 March 1808. William SHACKELFORD and Sally Suddeth. Minister, William Mason, Baptist. p 13

19 December 1811. Zachariah SHACKELFORD and Frances Lillard. Minister, Lewis Conner, Baptist. p 83

4 December 1804. Jacob SHANK and Rebecca Tobin. Minister, Charles Yates. p 21

2 November 1790. Robert SHELTON and Alpha Vawter. Minister, William Carpenter, Lutheran. p 81

16 December 1796. Jonathan SHINGLETON and Isabella Jett. Minister, John Swindler. p 81

18 June 1789. Ambrose SHIP and Nelly Barnes. Minister, William Mason, Baptist. p 80

5 May 1800. Michael SHORT and Esther Province. Minister, Frederick Kabler. p 82

8 January 1788. James SHOTWELL and Polly Crain. Minister, William Mason, Baptist. p 80

23 December 1802. Manson SIMMONS and Elizabeth Newton. Minister, William Mason, Baptist. p 82

11 January 1812. Hendley SIMPSON and Elizabeth Farrow. Minister, Lewis Conner, Baptist. p 83

22 January 1789. Abner SIMS and Mary Sanders. Minister, William Mason, Baptist. Mary, dau. John Sanders, will 2 November 1818; pro. 18 January 1819. p 80

15 September - . Benjamin SIMS and Anne Butler. Minister, Lewis Conner, Baptist. p 83

- - - . Caleb SIMS and Eleanor Poulter. Minister, Charles Yates. p 82

28 December 1809. Edmunds SIMS and Lavinia Tucker. Minister, William Mason, Baptist. p 15

22 December 1808. Henry SIMS and Peggy Marshall. Minister, William Mason, Baptist. p 16

29 December 1790. James SIMS and Jane Towles. Minister, William Mason, Baptist. p 81

4 January 1794. James SIMS and Patty Smith. Minister, Isham Tatum. p 80

17 February 1794. Jerry SIMS and Elizabeth Sanders. Minister, William Mason, Baptist. Elizabeth, dau. John Sanders, will 2 November 1818; pro. 18 January 1819. Spelled Jeremiah Sims in tax list. p 79

10 May 1796. John SIMS and Peggy Baxter. Minister, Charles Yates. p 79

26 May 1797. John SIMS and Peggy Baxter. Minister, Charles Yates. Both dates given. p 82

3 February 1805. Martin SIMS and Polly Wilhoit. Minister, Reuben Finnell. p 14

18 January 1787. Reuben SIMS and Sarah Tatum. Minister, William Mason, Baptist. p 80

22 December 1791. Robert SIMS and Polly Marston. Minister, Isham Tatum. p 79

25 October 1787. William SIMS and Mildred Baxter. Minister, William Mason, Baptist. p 80

6 February 1783. Alexander SIMSON and Ann Harrison. Minister, George Eve, Baptist. Spelled Simpson in tax list. p 79

27 January 1802. John SINE and Phebe Sine. Minister, Absalom Kinsey. p 83

30 October 1805. Allen SISK and Patsey Jenkins. Minister, Lewis Conner, Baptist. p 18

13 February 1787. Bartlett SISK and Mary Campbell. Minister, William Mason, Baptist. p 80

7 September 1786. Benjamin SISK and Elizabeth McCallaster. Minister, William Mason, Baptist. Green's Notes on Culpeper say McAllister. p 80

21 February 1799. Charles SISK and Nelly Chilton. Minister, Lewis Conner, Baptist. p 82

30 October 1795. George SISK and Nancy Chisem. Minister, Charles Yates. Green's Notes on Culpeper say Chishom. p 79

1 April 1813. John SISK and Elizabeth Fincham. Minister, Lewis Conner, Baptist. p 83

5 January 1790. Pluright SISK and Ruth Boone. Minister, William Mason, Baptist. p 81

3 January 1807. Benjamin SISSON and Elizabeth Brown. Minister, Reuben Finnell. New Index says Sesson. p 12

26 July 1798. Tarpley SISSON and Molly Pound. Minister, Nathaniel Sanders, Baptist. p 80

18 October 1798. William SISSON and Molly Brown. Minister, Frederick Kabler. p 83

21 October 1788. Elijah SKINNER and Elizabeth Jackson. Minister, George Eve, Baptist. p 79

25 July 1802. Steed SKINNER and Elener Brandone. Minister, Frederick Kabler. p 8

14 January 1802. William SKINNER and Betsey Trenton. Minister, William Mason, Baptist. p 82

4 November 1811. John SLAUGHTER and Sally Harper. Minister, Lewis Conner, Baptist. p 83

14 November 1799. Richard Y. SLAUGHTER and Mary B. Green. Minister, Reuben Finnell. p 82

21 November 1811. William SLAUGHTER and Frances H. Brown. Minister, Lewis Conner, Baptist. p 83

24 December 1813. William SLAUGHTER, Jr., and Harriet Ficklin. Minister, Lewis Conner, Baptist. p 83

6 December 1791. James SLEET and Rachel White. Minister, William Mason, Baptist. p 79

26 December 1802. Augustine SMITH and Ann Cosper. Minister, Absalom Kinsey. p 83

30 September 1784. Benjamin SMITH and Elizabeth Rogers. Minister, George Eve, Baptist. p 79

4 March 1800. Brisco SMITH and Jane Pratt. Minister, Isham Tatum. p 82

26 December 1799. Caleb SMITH and Jenny Scott. Minister, Absalom Kinsey. p 83

12 January 1792. Daniel SMITH and Jerusha Scott. Minister, William Mason, Baptist. p 79

7 April 1796. Daniel SMITH and Mary Colvin. Minister, William Mason, Baptist. p 80

20 August 1810. Hedgman SMITH and Betsy Cosper. Minister, Absolem King. p 20

4 February 1791. Isaac SMITH, Jr., and Susanna Smith. Minister, William Carpenter. p 81

5 October 1811. Isachar SMITH and Anne S. Calvert. Minister, Lewis Conner, Baptist. Anne Strother Calvert b. 1793 d. 1861, dau. Ralls and Mary Wade (Strother) Calvert; m. 15 November 1790. Isachar Smith b. 1791, d. 1842. She m. 2nd 1823 Henry Spiller. (Md. Hist. Mag. Vol. 16 p. 199). p 83

30 September 1796. Jesse SMITH and Joanna Pendleton. Minister, Nathaniel Pinckard. p 81

10 April 1794. Joel SMITH and Catherine Cosper. Minister, William Mason, Baptist. p 79

20 - 1803. Joel SMITH and Sarah Fincham. Minister, Lewis Conner, Baptist. p 17

23 January 1787. John SMITH and Elizabeth Raines. Minister, Nathaniel Sanders, Baptist. p 79

28 August 1788. John SMITH and Nancy Porter. Minister, William Mason, Baptist. p 80

15 August 1793. John SMITH and Elizabeth Loury. Minister, John Swindler. p 79

26 February 1798. John SMITH and Elizabeth Faye. Minister, Reuben Fennell. p 81

1 December 1803. John SMITH and Nancy Finks. Minister, William Mason, Baptist. p 9

7 June 1808. John SMITH and Sally Rush. Minister, William Mason, Baptist. p 13

26 October 1792. Martin SMITH and Tary Roberts. Minister, John Pickett, Baptist. p 82

24 July 1791. Michael SMITH and Rosanna Yager. Minister, William Carpenter, Lutheran. p 81

17 October 1793. Owen SMITH and Agnes Hill. Minister, John Swindler. p 81

6 April 1791. Robert SMITH, Jr., and Sally Watts. Minister, Nathaniel Sanders, Baptist. p 80

23 August 1814. Weedon SMITH and Lucy Browning. Minister, Lewis Conner, Baptist. p 83

8 August 1786. William SMITH and Lucy Wright. Minister, William Mason, Baptist. p 80

20 December 1792. William SMITH and Dinah Yager. Minister, William Carpenter, Jr., Lutheran. p 81

12 August 1793. William SMITH and Susanna Wicoff. Minister, John Hickerson, Baptist. p 82

13 October 1801. Gabriel SMITHER and Gilly Calvert. Minister, Reuben Finnell. Vol. I, p. 17 of the original Culpeper Marriage book says Gettie Calvert. She was dau. of John Calvert and his second wife, Helen Bailey. Born 1785. p 10

18 February 1808. John SMITHER and Mary Greenway. Minister, Lewis Conner, Baptist. p 20

17 October 1798. Alexander SMOOT and Ann Hawkins. Minister, Lewis Conner, Baptist. p 82

24 May 1799. Leonard SMOOT and Abigail Heaton. Minister, Charles Yates. p 79

4 December 1795. William SMOOT and Susanna Haden. Minister, John Pickett, Baptist. p 82

5 June 1798. John SMOTT and Anna Cannaday. Minister, John Hickerson, Baptist. This name is probably Smoot. Green's Notes on Culpeper say Smoot. p 81

3 January 1791. Aquilla SNAILING and Elizabeth Shotwell. Minister, William Mason, Baptist. p 81

6 September 1794. Fielding SNEDE and Elizabeth Crutcher. Minister, William Mason, Baptist. p 81

21 December 1788. David SNYDER and Martha Bryan. Minister, George Eve, Baptist. p 79

21 October 1783. John SNYDER and Winford Camble (Campbell?). Minister, William Mason, Baptist. Green's Notes on Culpeper say Campbell. p 80

7 September 1788. Joseph SNYDER and Mary Christopher. Minister, William Carpenter, Lutheran. p 79

16 February 1809. Joseph SNYDER and Sally Campbell. Minister, Lewis
Conner, Baptist. p 83

26 October 1815. Conway SPELMAN and Nancy Mason. Minister, William
Mason, Baptist. p 84

20 March 1787. Benjamin SPICER and Mary Towles. Minister, William
Mason, Baptist. p 80

12 November 1805. Cain SPICER and Elizabeth Lucas. Minister, William
Mason, Baptist. p 15

27 March 1798. Moses SPICER and Polly Moore. Minister, William Mason,
Baptist. p 80

5 January 1809. William SPILLER and Nancy Sullivan. Minister, Lewis
Conner, Baptist. p 83

15 September 1781. Thomas STANDLEY and Susanna Smith. Minister, George
Eve, Baptist. p 82

13 July 1803. Alexander STANFORD and Mary Adams. Minister, Charles
Yates. p 9

1 January 1793. James STARLING and Polly Norman. Minister, Lewis
Corbin. p 81

24 March 1796. William STAUNTON and Polly Moxley. Married at Dr. Dent's
in Fauquier. Minister, Rev. John Woodville, Rector of St. Mark's
Parish, Episcopal Church. St. Mark's Parish Register.

18 August 1798. Robert STEAL and Alice Taylor. Minister, Reuben
Fennell. p 81

10 January 1808. William STEPTOE and Elizabeth Cole. Minister, William
Mason, Baptist. p 13

17 May 1793. Robert STEVENS and Frances Rosson. Minister, William
Mason, Baptist. p 81

8 June 1799. William STEVENS and Caty Gore. Minister, Nathaniel
Sanders, Baptist. p 82

17 November 1786. James STEVENSON and Sarah Harden. Minister, John
Pickett, Baptist. p 79

17 January 1789. James STEVENSON and Susanna Hanback. Minister, John
Pickett, Baptist. p 79

3 March 1795. Samuel STEVENSON and Elizabeth Pierce. Minister, Lewis
Corbin. p 82

7 June 1796. Joseph STEWARD and Sarah Roberts. Minister, Isham Tatum. p 80

31 January 1793. John STEWART and Caty Campbell. Minister, Lewis Corbin. p 81

6 December 1800. Henry STIPES and Betsy Lampkin. Minister, Frederick Kabler. p 82

24 July 1788. Philip STOCKDELL and Sally Sampson. Minister, George Eve, Baptist. p 79

8 June 1791. William STOKES and Nancy Shaw. Minister, James Garnett, Baptist. p 79

10 January 1801. David STOKESBERRY and Frances Cocke. Minister, Frederick Kabler. p 82

21 February 1804. John STOKESBERRY and Sarah Cowgill. Minister, Frederick Kabler. p 10

15 November 1792. Ephraim STONESYVER and Julian Wilhoit. Minister, William Mason, Baptist. Also spelled Stonesever, Stonesypher, Stonesyfer and Stonesiffer. p 81

12 August 1790. John STONESYPHER and Mary Huffman. Minister, William Carpenter, Lutheran. Stonesever in tax list. p 81

16 July 1791. Francis STORY and Susanna Kelly. Minister, James Garnett, Baptist. p 79

16 March 1797. James STORY and Lucy Johnston. Minister, Lewis Conner, Baptist. p 82

2 December 1783. John STORY and Nancy Creel. Minister, William Mason, Baptist. p 80

9 April 1812. Russell STORY and Elizabeth Revercomb. Minister, Lewis Conner, Baptist. p 83

9 January 1790. William STORY and Elizabeth Yowell. Minister, William Mason, Baptist. p 81

27 October 1796. Jacob STOUT and Mildred Ballenger. Minister, William Mason, Baptist. p 81

30 May 1799. James STOUT and Abigail Holloway. Minister, Frederick Kabler. p 82

1 August 1784. Reuben STOUT and Mary Van Dike. Minister, William Mason, Baptist. p 80

8 February 1798. Elijah STOUTT and Elizabeth Turnham. Minister, William Mason, Baptist. Spelled Stout in tax list. p 80

19 July 1798. Peter STOUTT and Mary Sherwood. Minister, William Mason, Baptist. p 80

23 January 1794. Daniel STRINGER and Milly Green. Minister, Henry Fry. Milly, dau. Col. William and Ann (Coleman) Green. Ann Green's will dated 20 September 1804, pro. 15 Octber 1804. p 79

18 November 1813. French STROTHER and Mary Ann Browning. Minister, Lewis Conner, Baptist. p 83

28 February 1796. George STROTHER and Mary Duncan. Minister, Lewis Corbin. p 81

24 February 1804. John STROTHER and Sally Pendleton. Minister, Charles Yates. p 9

1 November 1814. John STROTHER and Elizabeth Brown. Minister, Lewis Conner, Baptist. p 84

12 October 1790. William STROTHER and Milly Medley. Minister, William Mason, Baptist. p 81

1 February 1810. Bailey SUDDOTH and Nancy Shackelford. Minister, William Mason, Baptist. p 15

13 July 1801. William SULLIVAN and Fanny Fewell. Minister, James Garnett, Baptist. p 10

21 July 1804. Hezekiah SUTER and Elizabeth Brown. Minister, Frederick Kabler. p 10

13 February 1795. Elisha SUTTLE and Aggy Miller. Minister, Lewis Corbin. p 82

23 Feburary 1803. Thomas SUTTON and Mildred Zimmerman. Minister, William Mason, Baptist. p 82

30 July 1786. George SWINDLE and Catherine Rasor. Minister, George Eve, Baptist. p 79

21 April 1790. George SWINDLE and Hannah Cornelius. Minister, James Garnett, Baptist. p 81

21 June 1810. Clayton SWINDLER and Sally Bryant. Minister, Lewis Conner, Baptist. p 83

-    - -. Henry SWINDLER and Peggy Boston. Minister, Charles Yates. p 82

29 December 1797. John SWINDLER, Jr., and Rachel Fryer. Minister, John Swindler. p 81

19 February 1800. Henry TALIAFERRO and Elizabeth Lovell. Minister, William Mason, Baptist. p 88

12 March 1795. John TALIAFERRO and Alice Luckie. Minister, John Woodville, Rector of St. Mark's Parish, Episcopal Church. Married at Capt. Henry Taliaferro's. p 87

6 May 1811. William TALIAFERRO and Nancy Tutt. Minister, Lewis Conner, Baptist. Nancy, dau. of John Tutt, will 8 May 1812; pro. 15 June 1812. p 89

29 May 1814. William TANNEHILL and Henrietta Fogg. Minister, William Northam. p 89

22 March 1791. John TANNER and Susanna Good. Minister, William Carpenter, Lutheran. p 88

23 December 1813. John TANNER and Jane Collins. Minister, Jesse Butler. p 89

28 January 1787. William TATE and Ann West. Minister, George Eve, Baptist. p 87

21 December 1797. William TATUM and Polly Lucas. Minister, William Mason, Baptist. p 87

30 December 1791. Edmond TAYLOR and Elizabeth Utz. Minister, William Mason, Baptist. p 87

30 July 1799. George TAYLOR and Sally Fishback. Minister, John Hickerson, Baptist. p 88

20 May 1798. James TAYLOR and Elizabeth Atkins. Minister, Charles Yates. p 88

22 January 1815. John TAYLOR and Catherine Harvey. Minister, James Withers, Baptist. p 89

18 August 1782. Henry TELPH and Ann Powell. Minister, George Eve, Baptist. p 87

20 October 1806. Joel TERRELL and Lucy Marshall. Minister, William Mason, Baptist. p 12

20 April 1789. John TERRELL and Rebecca Cornelius. Minister, James Garnett, Baptist. p 87

23 November 1805. Micajah TERREL and Charlotte Appleby. Minister, James Garnett, Baptist. p 15

- June 1814. William TERRELL and Lydia Coffman. Minister, James Boyd. p 89

16 December 1797. Thomas THATCHER and Jane Menefee. Minister, John Pickett, Baptist. p 88

9 April 1812. Nathaniel THREAD and Nelly Campbell. Minister, Lewis Conner, Baptist. p 89

4 March 1814. George S. THOM and Mary L. Waugh. Minister, Henry Fry. p 89

31 December 1797. James A. THOM and Alice Taliaferro. Minister, Rev. John Woodville, Rector of St. Mark's Parish, Episcopal Church. See James A. Thorn. St. Mark's Parish Register.

28 November 1805. Mitcheal THOM and Mary Calvert. Minister, Reuben Finnell. Mary Calvert b. 1780, d. 1809, dau. of George Calvert 1712-1782 by his 2nd wife, Mary (Strother) Deatherage, m. 1779. See Mitchal Thorne. p 14

23 January 1799. Benjamin THOMAS and Elizabeth Gaines. Minister, Lewis Conner, Baptist. Elizabeth, dau. of Richard Gaines will 27 July 1802; pro. 18 February 1805. p 88

14 September 1803. Elijah THOMAS and Nancy Hughes. Minister, Lewis Conner, Baptist. p 17

28 December 1788. Elisha THOMAS and Leanna Zigler. Minister, William Mason, Baptist. p 87

20 December 1785. Massey THOMAS and Elizabeth Barbour. Minister, William Mason, Baptist. p 87

24 November 1808. Nesley THOMAS and Mary Hughes. Minister, Lewis Conner, Baptist. p 20

15 December 1790. John THOMPSON and Mildred Raines. Minister, George Eve, Baptist. p 87

28 November 1793. Joseph THOMPSON and Joanna Hale. Minister, Nathaniel Pinckard. p 87

20 January 1813. Martin THOMPSON and Rebecca Foster. Minister, William Mason, Baptist. p 89

29 November 1794. Thomas THOMPSON and Frances Ross. Minister, Frederick Kabler. p 88

2 December 1802. Walter THOMPSON and Isabel Brown. Minister, Lewis Conner, Baptist. p 88

22 December 1814. William F. THOMPSON and Elizabeth Strother. Minister, Lewis Conner, Baptist. p 89

31 December 1787. James A. THORN and Alice Taliaferro. Minister, Rev. John Woodville, Rector of St. Mark's Parish, Episcopal Church. See James A. Thom. St. Mark's Parish Register.

28 November 1805. Mitchal THORNE and Mary Calvert. Minister, Reuben Finnell. See Mitcheal Thom. This marriage has been checked by the original and could be either Thom or Thorne. p 14

20 December 1802. Joseph THORNHILL and Sally Westall. Minister, William Mason, Baptist. p 9

16 January 1812. Joseph THORNHILL and Elizabeth Butler. Minister, Lewis Conner, Baptist. p 89

6 August 1796. Reuben THORNHILL and Sally Shingleton. Minister, Lewis Conner, Baptist. p 88

9 August 1796. Reuben THORNHILL and Sally Shingleton. Minister, Lewis Conner, Baptist. Both marriages given on same page. p 88

30 June 1791. Benjamin THORNTON and Ann Piner. Minister, James Garnett, Baptist. p 87

11 April 1790. James THORNTON and Sally Hawkins. Minister, Isham Tatum. p 87

18 July 1799. Daniel THRELKELD and Lucy Duncan. Minister, William Mason, Baptist. Lucy, dau. of James Duncan, will 17 August 1801; estate divided August 1819. p 88

29 June 1784. James THRELKELD and Ann Kelly. Minister, William Mason, Baptist. p 87

7 May 1789. James THRELKELD and Polly Casper. Minister, William Mason, Baptist. p 87

10 June 1794. James THRELKELD and Elizabeth Garner. Minister, William Mason, Baptist. p 87

6 October 1811. John THRELKELD and Patsy Furgeson. Minister, William Mason, Baptist. p 89

19 March 1795. Moses THRELKELD and Sarah Whitehead. Minister, William Mason, Baptist. p 87

6 February 1804. Catlett TIFFEE and Frances Asher. Minister, Frederick Kabler. p 10

10 March 1782. William TINSLEY and Frances Rogers. Minister, George Eve, Baptist. p 87

5 April 1811. Isaac TOBIN and Winny Shackelford. Minister, Lewis Conner, Baptist. p 89

9 March 1801. Nathan TOBIN and Sally Condy. Minister, James Garnett, Baptist. p 10

26 November 1801. Christian TOMLIN and Lucy Wright. Minister, Reuben Finnell. p 11

5 November 1801. William TOMLIN and Sarah Wright. Minister, Reuben Finnell. p 10

17 September 1798. Robert TOOMBS and Sally Catlett. Minister, Frederick Kabler. p 88

19 December 1809. George TOWLES and Frances Mason. Minister, George Mason, Baptist. p 17

23 November 1815. George TOWLES and Elizabeth Bowers. Minister, William Mason, Baptist. p 90

29 March 1792. Henry TOWLES and Uphias Tucker. Minister, William Mason, Baptist. p 87

16 February 1786. Joseph TOWLES and Polly Witherall. Minister, John Price, Baptist. p 87

21 June 1798. James TRIGGER and Polly Green. Minister, John Hickerson, Baptist. p 88

31 March 1814. Alfred TRIPLETT and Ann Odor. Minister, Robert Jones, Baptist. p 89

3 February 1791. Daniel TRIPLETT and Susanna Botts. Minister, William Mason, Baptist. p 88

26 May 1788. Hedgman TRIPLETT and Molly McClanahan. Minister, John Pickett, Baptist. p 87

21 December 1810. Allen TUCKER and Polly Maury. Minister, William Mason, Baptist. p 15

6 June 1798. John TUCKER and Nancy Tobin. Minister, Lewis Conner, Baptist. p 88

27 May 1812. John TUCKER and Clarissa B. Smith. Minister, William Mason, Baptist. p 89

17 February 1801. Littleton TUCKER and Rachel Threlkeld. Minister, John West. p 88

19 March 1793. Moses. TUCKER and Usley Goodman. Minister, William Mason, Baptist. p 87

23 December 1800. Stephen TUCKER and Elizabeth Crawley. Minister, John West. p 88

24 November 1808. Thomas TUCKER and Nancy Sims. Minister, William Mason, Baptist. Green's Notes on Culpeper say Simms. p 16

22 May 1798. William TUCKER and Jemima Lewis. Minister, Lewis Mason, Baptist. p 87

10 November 1812. John TUCKWILLER and Polly Edwards. Minister, Lewis Conner, Baptist. p 89

26 December 1799. Armistead TURNER and Molly Kennady. Minister, Frederick Kabler. p 88

27 August 1789. Benjamin TURNER and Agatha Watts. Minister, George Eve, Baptist. p 88

24 December 1812. Cornelius TURNER and Susanna Colvin. Minister, William Mason, Baptist. p 89

13 April 1815. Daniel TURNER and Milly Bryan. Minister, Lewis Conner, Baptist. p 89

8 March 1805. James TURNER and Betsey Turner. Minister, Reuben Finnell. p 14

15 September 1807. James TURNER and Delphia Garner. Minister, Lewis Conner, Baptist. p 19

2 December 1792. Joshua TURNER and Mary Corley. Minister, John Pickett, Baptist. p 88

18 July 1803. Larkin TURNER and Peggy Kline. Minister, Frederick Kabler. p 8

21 August 1801. Leonard TURNER and Sally Campbell. Minister, Absalom King. p 88

20 February 1806. Martin TURNER and Hannah Marshall. Minister, William Mason, Baptist. p 16

8 September 1803. Rawley TURNER and Nancy Hopper. Minister, William Mason, Baptist. p 9

13 May 1802. Richard TURNER and Frances Hume. Minister, William Mason, Baptist. p 88

3 January 1793. Samuel TURNER and Abigail Haines. Minister, William Mason, Baptist. p 87

27 February 1800. Zepheniah TURNER and Sally M. Conner. Minister, William Mason, Baptist. p 88

31 March 1812. Gabriel TUTT and Milly Menefee. Minister, William Mason, Baptist. p 89

23 October 1800. James L. TUTT and Lucy Finks. Minister, Absalom Kinsey. p 88

3 December 1812. Richard Elzey TUTT and Matilda C. Royster. Minister, Lewis Conner, Baptist. p 89

1 December 1795. Richard J. TUTT and Milly Conner. Minister, William Mason, Baptist. p 87

23 August 1787. Thomas TUTT and Sally Parks. Minister, William Mason, Baptist. p 87

2 October 1792. William TUTT and Winny Pulliam. Minister, William Mason, Baptist. p 87

9 January 1790. George TWYMAN and Ann Twyman. Minister, George Eve, Baptist. p 88

22 October 1801. James TYE and Franky Collins. Minister, Frederick Kabler. p 88

1 October 1782. Joseph UNDERWOOD and Winney Henderson. Minister, George Eve, Baptist. p 91

23 December 1799. Daniel UPDIKE and Ruth Heaton. Minister, Charles Yates. p 91

12 October 1809. Thompson UTTERBACK and Betsey Vaughan. Minister, William Mason, Baptist. p 17

7 July 1791. Absalom UTZ and Anne Cook. Minister, William Carpenter, Lutheran. p 91

23 December 1788. John UTZ and Elizbeth Christler. Minister, William Carpenter, Lutheran. p 91

30 November 1790. Lewis UTZ and Mary Carpenter. Minister, William Carpenter. p 91

10 December 1791. Peter VAN DYKE and Anne Stout. Minister, William Mason, Baptist. p 91

9 June 1814. Jesse VAN HORN and Elizabeth Pulliam. Minister, Lewis Conner, Baptist. p 91

8 December 1808. Jeremiah VAUGHAN and May Green. Minister, Absalom Kinsey. p 17

17 December 1807. John VAUGHAN and Peggy Tobin. Minister, Lewis Conner, Baptist. p 19

31 August 1797. Peter VAUGHAN and Sarah Beazley. Minister, Rev. John Woodville, Rector of St. Mark's Parish, Episcopal Church. St. Mark's Parish Register.

29 December 1791. Russell VAUGHAN and Elizabeth Hill. Minister, Nathaniel Sanders, Baptist. p 91

22 March 1781. Jesse VAUGHTER and Elizabeth Watts. Minister, Elijah Craig, Baptist. p 91

27 October 1790. Anthony VERNON and Frances Guinn. Minister, George Eve, Baptist. Old Index say Quinn. p 91

29 April 1802. James VINCE and Janny Gore. Minister, Reuben Finnell. p 11

9 November 1803. Frederick VISCARVER and Frances Browning. Minister, Lewis Conner, Baptist. p 17

9 May 1794. Nicholas VOSS and Mary Spotswood. Married at Col. Spotswood's. Minister, Rev. John Woodville, Rector of St. Mark's Parish, Episcopal Church. St. Mark's Parish Register.

20 December 1792. William WADDLE and Elizabeth Haywood. Minister, William Mason, Baptist. p 93

27 March 1786. Greensby WAGGONER and Sarah Mitchell. Minister, John Price, Baptist. p 93

4 October 1786. Thomas WAGGONER and Mary Garnett. Minister, Thomas Ammon, Baptist. p 92

6 February 1787. George WAITE and Mary Haynes. Minister, Isham Tatum. p 92

24 November 1803. Adam WALAND and Juda Burke. Minister, William Mason, Baptist. p 9

26 December 1805. John WALBRIDGE and Milly Hendrick. Minister, William Mason, Baptist. p 16

11 December 1794. Thomas WALDEN and Lucy Hughes. Minister, William Mason, Baptist. p 93

12 March 1807. Peter WALDRIDGE and Fanny Blackwell. Minister, William Mason, Baptist. p 13

24 November 1791. Lawson WALE and Lucy Thornton. Minister, James Garnett. Baptist. p 94

22 November 1808. - WALKER and Polly Berry. Minister, Absalom Kinsey. p 17

4 April 1793. James WALKER and Jemima Yager. Minister, William Carpenter, Lutheran. p 94

19 April 1792. Benjamin WALL and Lucy Pinnell. Minister, William Wright. p 92

26 August 1790. Richard WALL and Sucky Vernon. Minister, George Eve, Baptist. p 94

11 February 1798. William WALL and Caty Morgan. Minister, Reuben Finnell. p 93

18 December 1806. William WALLACE and Eliza Yates. Minister, Lewis Conner, Baptist. p 19

27 February 1787. Robert WALLE and Fanny Passons. Minister, William Mason, Baptist. p 93

-    -   -. William WALLE and Mary Walle. Minister, Charles Yates. p 94

4 February 1795. Oliver WALLIS and Hannah Wright. Minister, William Mason, Baptist. p 93

7 April 1791. William WALLIS and Mildred Walker. Minister, William Carpenter, Lutheran. p 94

23 December 1788. John WALLS and Fanny Sebree. Minister, George Eve, Baptist. p 92

12 December 1799. Elias WALTERS and Sally Gaunt. Minister, Absalom Kinsey. p 94

30 January 1788. Jacob WARD and Sally Quinn. Minister, George Eve, Baptist. p 92

10 December 1789. James WARD and Frances Jenkins. Minister, William Mason, Baptist. p 94

19 December 1782. William WARD and Sarah Vernon. Minister, George Eve, Baptist. p 92

24 December 1802. William WARD and Frances Browning. Minister, Reuben Finnell. p 11

25 June 1805. William WARD and Polly W. Strother. Minister, Lewis Conner, Baptist. p 18

27 September 1792. Moses WASHBOURN and Agatha Ethenton. Minister, Lewis Corbin. p 93

4 January 1787. William WATERS and Mary Brown. Minister, John Price, Baptist. p 93

5 May 1788. Robert WATTS and Susanna Lewis. Minister, Nathaniel Sanders, Baptist. p 93

18 December 1781. Joshua WAYLAND and Rachel Utz. Minister, George Eve, Baptist. p 93

16 February 1792. Joshua WAYLAND and Anne Ward. Minister, William Carpenter, Lutheran. p 93

1 April 1792. Harman WAYMAN and Frances Clore. Minister, William Mason, Baptist. p 92

18 April 1804. Francis WEAKLEY and Mary Berry. Minister, Lewis Conner, Baptist. p 17

10 May 1814. William WEAKLEY and Susan Sisk. Minister, Lewis Conner, Baptist. p 95

22 December 1791. Matthias WEAVER and Eleanor Wayland. Minister, William Carpenter, Lutheran. p 93

10 April 1788. Augustine WEBB and Lucy Crittenden. Minister, Isham Tatum. p 95

18 - 1799. Caleb WEBB and Fanny Gosney. Minister, James Garnett, Baptist. p 94

8 January 1807. Lewis WEBB and Nelly Threlkeld. Minister, William Mason, Baptist. p 13

30 November 1795. Augustine WEEDEN and Elizabeth Farmer. Minister, John Hickerson, Baptist. p 94

9 December 1794. William WEEKS and Ann Adams. Minister, Charles Yates. p 92

26 November 1795. Isaiah WELCH and Agnes Hawkins. Minister, John Swindler. p 94

2 January 1787. William WHALEY and Nancy Pulham. Minister, William Mason, Baptist. p 93

16 November 1804. Beverly WHARTON and Judith Clatterbuck. Minister, Lewis Conner, Baptist. p 17

3 January 1805. John WHARTON and Nancy Butler. Minister, Lewis Conner, Baptist. p 17

18 December 1800. Daniel WHEATLEY and Susanna Cooper. Minister, Absalom Kinsey. p 95

29 March 1792. William WHEATLEY and Susanna Grigsby. Minister, Stephen G. Roszel, Methodist. p 94

21 July 1794. George WHEELER and Lydia Calvert. Minister, John Pickett, Baptist. Lydia b. 1777, dau. of George And Lydia Beck (Ralls) Calvert, m. 7 November 1764. p 92

7 December 1792. John WHEELER and Alice Harford. Minister, William Wright. p 92

5 June 1783. Galen WHITE and Mildred Alexander. Minister, George Eve, Baptist. p 92

4 October 1810. James J. WHITE and Ann Buckham. Minister, Daniel James. p 21

9 August 1790. Jeremiah WHITE and Rachel Herndon. Minister, George Eve, Baptist. p 94

25 March 1790. John WHITE and Lucy Waggoner. Minister, James Garnett, Baptist. p 94

18 November 1807. Reuben WHITE and Polly Parsons. Minister, Reuben Finnell. p 14

6 September 1788. Thomas WHITE and Elizabeth Graves. Minister, William Mason, Baptist. p 93

30 September 1794. John WHITEHEAD and Elizabeth Routt. Minister, William Mason, Baptist. p 93

18 June 1801. John WHITEHEAD and Margaret Payton. Minister, James Garnett, Baptist. Green's Notes on Culpeper say Peyton. p 10

27 December 1792. Nelson WHITEHEAD and Elizabeth Coleman. Minister, William Mason, Baptist. p 93

12 November 1791. Vincent WHITEHEAD and Elizabeth Clifton. Minister, William Mason, Baptist. p 92

- November 1804. Cornelius WHITESCARVER and Elizabeth Browning. Minister, Reuben Finnell. p 14

23 September 1809. Robert WHITESCARVER and Sally Browning. Minister, Lewis Conner, Baptist. p 95

16 February 1789. John WHITESIDES and Caty Coons. Minister, John Pickett, Baptist. p 93

30 May 1811. William G. WIATT and Frances Levell. Minister, Isham Tatum. p 21

25 March 1795. John WIGGINTON and Mary M. Bell. Minister, John Woodville, Rector of St. Mark's Parish, Episcopal Church. Married at Captain Slaugher's. p 94

20 March 1794. John WILHOIT and Jenny Story. Minister, William Mason, Baptist. p 93

11 September 1787. Lewis WILHOIT and Rosanna Blankenbaker. Minister, William Carpenter, Lutheran. p 92

24 December 1789. Michael WILHOIT and Jemima Lucas. Minister, William Mason, Baptist. p 94

25 December 1789. Moses WILHOIT and Anne Hume. Minister, Isham Tatum. p 95

-    -   1815. Reynolds WILHOIT and Lucy Towles. Green's Notes on Culpeper. p 73

28 October 1787. William WILHOIT and Anna Clore. Minister, William Carpenter, Lutheran. p 92

3 March 1806. William WILHOIT and Elizabeth Weaver. Minister, William Mason, Baptist. p 16

-    -   1794. William WILKS and Anne Adams. Green's Notes on Culpeper. p 73

-    -   1809. Alexander WILLIAMS and Nancy Price. Minister, Abraham Kersey. p 12

21 May 1795. Joseph WILLIAMS and Elizabeth Settle. Minister, John Hickerson, Baptist. p 94

19 May 1799. Thomas R. WILLIAMS and Marreen Brown. Minister, Nathaniel Sanders, Baptist. Green's Notes on Culpeper say Marion. p 93

7 October 1806. Thomas WILLIAMSON and Mary Mozingo. Minister, Lewis Conner, Baptist. p 18

16 January 1794. Charles WILLIS and Lucy Shelton. Minister, William Mason, Baptist. p 93

8 January 1787. Edward WILLIS and Frances Towles. Minister, William Mason, Baptist. p 93

25 October 1784. John WILLIS and Jane Dogan. Minister, Isham Tatum. p 92

22 December 1802. John WILLIS and Edna Bragg. Minister, Frederick Kabler. p 8

9 January 1815. Joshua WILLIS and Arcy Willis. Minister, James Garnett, Baptist. p 95

3 July 1791. Moses WILLIS and Susanna White. Minister, James Garnett, Baptist. p 92

18 November 1793. Isaac WILLSON and Elizabeth Cook. Minister, John Pickett, Baptist. p 92

22 May 1798. Isaac WILSON and Anna Garnett. Minister, James Garnett, Baptist. p 94

16 November 1790. Samuel WILSON and Nancy Sutherland. Minister, John Pickett, Baptist. p 94

24 August 1802. Thomas WINDSOR and Lydia Hasby. Minister, Reuben Finnell. p 11

29 January 1806. James WISE and Sally Ethington. Minister, William Mason, Baptist. p 16

27 July 1797. John WISE and Dolly Morriss. Minister, William Mason, Baptist. p 93

31 March 1793. Manning WISE and Elizabeth Barbour. Minister, William Mason, Baptist. p 94

- May 1815. William WISE and Lucy Etherton. Minister, William Mason, Baptist. p 95

21 October 1790. Peter WITHAM and Mary Dicken. Minister, Isham Tatum. p 94

18 December 1788. John WITHERALL and Elizabeth Chapman. Minister, William Mason, Baptist. p 93

23 July 1799. Elijah WITHERS and Jemimah Hudnell. Minister, John Pickett, Baptist. p 95

21 February 1794. Matthew K. WITHERS and Catherine Spencer. Minister, John Pickett, Baptist. K. for Keene? p 94

29 November 1786. Peter WOMACK and Crissey Utterback. Minister, John Pickett, Baptist. p 91

30 June 1808. Alexander WOMAX and Jamijah Steptoe. Minister, Absalom Kinsey. p 17

23 February 1790. William WOOD and Mary Ann Clark. Minister, John Pickett, Baptist. p 94

27 July 1811. Charles WOODARD and Sally Hisle. Minister, Lewis Conner, Baptist. p 95

14 November 1815. Charles WOODARD and Nancy Frazier. Minister, Lewis Conner, Baptist. p 95

11 January 1810. George WOODARD and Nancy Chilton. Minister, Lewis Conner, Baptist. p 95

26 March 1800. James WOODARD and Anne Young. Minister, Charles Yates. p 94

29 September 1815. John WOODARD and Polly Martin. Minister, Lewis Conner, Baptist. p 95

9 October 1808. Joseph WOODARD and Betsey Bowling. Minister, Lewis Conner, Baptist. p 20

1 February 1791. William WOODARD and Susanna Hisle. Minister, William Mason, Baptist. p 94

20 December 1793. William WOODARD and Anne Barnhisel. Minister, John Swindler. p 94

14 October 1788. James WOTHERSPON and Mary Gin. Minister, William Mason, Baptist. p 93

22 December 1796. Charles WRIGHT and Polly Holmes. Minister, John Swindler. p 93

10 September 1801. Charles D. WRIGHT and Lucy Mason. Minister, Lewis Conner, Baptist. p 95

16 January 1809. John WRIGHT and Frency (?) Corbin. Minister, William Mason, Baptist. p 16

19 January 1792. Morgan WRIGHT and Elizabeth Threlkeld. Minister, William Mason, Baptist. p 92

2 June 1813. Nathaniel WRIGHT and Clary Baldrich. Minister, Lewis Conner, Baptist. p 95

21 November 1793. Richard WRIGHT and Anne Story. Minister, William Mason, Baptist. p 93

5 June 1799. Richard WRIGHT and Ann Smith. Minister, William Mason, Baptist. p 94

9 October 1792. Adam YAGER and Ann Dicken. Minister, William Mason, Baptist. p 97

5 January 1790. Benjamin YAGER and Anna Christler. Minister, William Carpenter, Lutheran. p 97

18 December 1786. Elisha YAGER and Elizabeth Yager. Minister, William Yager. p 97

20 January 1791. Ephraim YAGER and Sarah Rodlheifer. Minister, William Carpenter, Lutheran. p 97

19 December 1786. John YAGER and Hannah Yager. Minister, William Mason, Baptist. p 97

1 January 1790. John YAGER and Anne Carpenter. Minister, William Carpenter, Lutheran. p 97

3 November 1791. John YAGER and Markaret Wilhoit. Minister, Isham Tatum. p 97

5 September 1809. John YAGER and Anna Kabler. Minister, Henry Fry. p 15

16 October 1806. Joseph YAGER and Sally Chick or Chich. Minister, William Mason, Baptist. p 12

4 November 1789. Nathaniel YAGER and Betsy Hudson. Minister, Isham Tatum. p 97

22 December 1785. Nicholas YAGER and Anne Wayland. Minister, Isham Tatum. p 97

16 March 1790. Nicholas YAGER and Memima Yager. Minister, William Carpenter, Lutheran. p 97

1 November 1803. Birkett G. YANCEY and Milley Menefee. Minister, Lewis Conner, Baptist. p 17

15 November 1792. Ludwell YANCY and Elizabeth Jeffries. Minister, William Mason, Baptist. Elizabeth, dau. of James Jeffries, will 29 June 1805; pro. 16 December 1805. p 97

31 December 1795. Abner YATES and Clara Smith. Minister, William Mason, Baptist. p 97

3 December 1803. Benjamin YATES and Alice Finnell. Minister, Reuben Finnell. p 11

4 February 1813. Boswell P. YATES and Clarissa A. Gaines. Minister, William Mason, Baptist. Clarissa, dau. of James Gaines, will 10 October 1805; pro. 21 October 1805. p 97

10 April 1798. Francis YATES and Peggy Hughes. Minister, Charles Yates. p 97

14 December 1815. Garrett YATES and Frances Yates. Minister, Lewis Conner, Baptist. p 98

28 November 1793. George YATES and Elizabeth Browning. Minister, William Mason, Baptist. p 97

25 December 1800. George YATES and Polly Browning. Minister, James Garnett, Baptist. p 10

31 December 1789. Warner YATES and Elizabeth Baxter. Minister, William Mason, Baptist. p 97

13 February 1786. William YATES and Isabella Gaines. Minister, William Mason, Baptist. p 97

3 June 1813. William YATES and Elizabeth Lillard. Minister, Lewis Conner, Baptist. p 98

20 March 1809. Benjamin YOUNG and Mary Williams. Minister, William Mason, Baptist. p 16

11 January 1789. Charles YOUNG and Sally Mayer. Minister, George Eve, Baptist. p 97

11 March 1786. Samuel YOUNG and Mary Coons. Minister, John Pickett, Baptist. This marriage is given twice, one date 8 March 1786. p 97

4 January 1789. Samuel YOUNG and Margaret Rogers. Minister, George Eve, Baptist. p 97

17 March 1808. Mery YOWELL and Sally Chilton. Minister, Lewis Conner, Baptist. p 20

27 December 1791. William YOWELL and Lucy Ship. Minister, William Carpenter, Lutheran. p 97

6 December 1787. William ZACARY and Ann Rice. -?. William Zachary in tax list. p 100

6 February 1794. Daniel ZIMMERMAN and Mary Carter. Minister, William Mason, Baptist. p 100

22 March 1791. John ZIMMERMAN and Elizabeth Fewel. Minister, William Mason, Baptist. p 100

28 April 1791. Michael ZIMMERMAN and Elizabeth Hufman. -?. p 100

6 March 1783. Reuben ZIMMERMAN and Elizabeth Zigler. Minister, William Mason, Baptist. p 100

ABBOTT,
Susanna 75
ADAMS,
Ann 95
Anne 97
Elizabeth 24, (2) 49
Jane 21, 64
Mary 84
Sarah 16
ALEXANDER,
Lucy 16
Mildred 96
ALLEN,
Ann 73
Judy 45
Mary 71
ALSOP,
Dolly 34
Polly 69
AMISS,
Elizabeth 29
ANDERSON,
Nancy 18
Rebecca 72
ANTRIM,
Sarah 26
APPLEBEE - APPLEBY,
Charlotte 87
Jane 47
Sarah 39
ARNOLD,
Letty 48
ASHER,
Frances 89
Nancy 71
Sally 20
Sarah 7
ASKINS,
Ann 16
ATKINS,
Elizabeth 87
Lucy 8
ATWOOD,
Anne 24
AYNES,
Jane 41

BAHAUGHAN,
Susanna 54
BAKER,
Sarah 49
BALANCE,
Patty 42
Polly 42
BALDRICH,
Clary 100
BALL,
Judith 45
BALLARD,
Elizabeth 34
Molly 34
BALLENGER - BALLINGER,
Mildred 85
Polly 16
Sally 45
BANKS,
Lizzie 49
BANSELL,
Susanna 75
BARBER - BARBOUR,
Ann 35
Elizabeth 88, 98
BARLER,
Anne 41
BARNES,
Caty 49
Mary 34
Nelly 79
Patty 56
Sally 34
Tomson 56

BARNHISEL,
Anne 99
BASEY - BASYE,
Catharine 5, 78
BATES,
Frances 51
BAUGHN,
Keziah 77
BAXTER,
Elizabeth 101
Mildred 80
Peggy (2) 80
Phoebe 41
BEASLEY,
Sarah 93
BECKHAM,
Frances 59
Mary 72
BELL,
Eleanor C. 38
Mary M. 97
BENGHAM,
Jane 2
BENNETT,
Rebecca 9
BERRY,
Betsey 14
Lucy 6
Mary 95
Polly 94
Sarah 54
BIFFY,
Elizabeth 49
BIGBEE,
Lydia 29
BINGHAM,
Rebecca 39
BISHOP,
Mary 61
Patience 50
BLACKBURN,
Martha 32
BLACKWELL,
Catherine 15
Fanny 94
BLAIR,
Anne 23
BLANKENBAKER,
Peggy 19
Rosanna 97
BOLING - BOWLING,
Betsy 99
Sally 44
BOON - BOONE,
Hannah 4
Ruth 81
BORDEN,
Peggy 66
BORN,
Polly 66
BOSTON,
Peggy 86
BOSTS,
Nancy 54
BOSWELL,
Fanny 61
Sally 10
BOTTS,
Frances 27
Nancy 21
Susanna 90
BOUGHAN,
Keziah 71
BOUGHORN,
Sarah 3
BOURN,
Susanna 67
BOWEN,
Nancy 6
BOWERS,
Elizabeth 90

BRADY,
Elizabeth 38
Mary 42
BRAGG,
Edna 98
Polly 11
BRANDOM,
Lucy 6
BRANDON - BRANDONE,
Elener 81
Lucy 6
Polly 40
BRANHAM,
Nancy 37
Nelly 39
BRARINHAN -BRANHAM,
Catherine 43
BREEDLOVE,
Fanny 39
Nancy 35
BRIDWELL,
Polly 44
BROADUS,
Caty G. 15
BROWN,
Agnes 48
Anne 29
Elizabeth 49, 71, 78,
81, (2) 86
Frances 4
Frances H. 81
Hannah 30
Isabel 88
Keziah 72
Kitty 27
Letty 18
Lilly 18
Lucy 58, 59
Marion 97
Marreen 97
Mary 50, 95
Molly 81
Peggy F. 50
Phoebe 12
Polly 60
Sally (2) 62
BROWNING,
Elizabeth 30, 97, 101
Frances 93, 95
Lucy 13, 30, 83
Malinda 13
Mary 13
Mary Ann 86
Nancy 30
Polly 101
Sally 65, 97
Siney 53
BROYLE,
Frances 66
Rosanna 38
BRUCE,
Elizabeth 48
Mary 21
BRYAN,
Martha 83
Milly 91
Phebe 40
Ruth 59
BRYANT,
Sally 86
BUCKHAM,
Sally 96
BUMGARNER - BUMGARDNER,
Dibly 72
Elizabeth 75
Susanna 38
BUNGARD,
Margaret 48
BURBRIDGE,
Betsey 2

BURGESS,
  Elizabeth 50
BURK - BURKE - BURKS,
  Jane 72
  Juda 93
  Nancy 28
  Susanna 19
BURNS,
  Molly 58
BURRIS,
  Mildred 74
BURTON,
  Elizabeth 33
BUTLER,
  Anne 79
  Dorcas 30
  Eleanor 3
  Elizabeth 89
  Hannah 11
  Isabel 32
  Nancy 15, 96
  Polly 54, 57, 70
  Sarah 37
  Susanna 32
BUTT - BUTTS,
  Eleanor 22
  Elizabeth 38
  Rosamond 9
BYWATERS,
  Delena 63
  Edy 34
  Elizabeth 13
  Lucy 30
  Nancy 25

C--,
  Mary 12
CALLAHAN,
  Mary 58
CALVERT,
  Anne 16, 26
  Anne Strother 82
  Elizabeth 67
  Getty 83
  Gilly 83
  Hannah 59
  Jane 26
  Lydia 96
  Margaret 1
  Maria 65
  Mary 88, 89
  Nancy 16
  Sarah 43, 44, 55
CAMP,
  Elizabeth 22, 77
CAMPBELL - CAMBLE,
  Caty 85
  Lucy 12, 17
  Mary 17, 80
  Milly 70
  Nancy 27
  Nelly 88
  Sally 84, 91
  Susanna 37
  Winford 83
CANADAY - CANNADAY,
  Anna 83
  Elizabeth 10
CANNON,
  Elizabeth 17
  Peggy 57
CARDER,
  Caty 6
  Lucy 11
  Milly 50
  Patty 6
  Polly 18
CARDWELL,
  Nancy 12
CARPENTER,
  Anne 100
  Elizabeth 8
  Mary 92

CARPENTER (Continued),
  Rebecca 63
  Sally 44
  Susanna 52
CARTER,
  Mary 102
  Mary Ann 4
CASEY,
  Eleanor 70
CASPER,
  Polly 89
CATLETT,
  Sally 90
CAVE,
  Sally Muse 19
CHAPMAN,
  Elizabeth 98
  Sarah 1
CHAMBERS,
  Peggy 64
CHANDLER,
  Nancy 53
CHART,
  Susan 44
CHEEK,
  Milly 51
CHESTER,
  Mary 19
CHEWNING - CHOWNING,
  Elizabeth (2) 73
CHICK,
  Elizabeth 48
  Sally 100
CHILTON,
  Betty 1
  Catherine 29
  Judith 29
  Nancy 99
  Nelly 80
  Sally 101
CHISEM - CHISHOM,
  Nancy 80
CHRISTLER,
  Anne 100
  Elizabeth 92
CHRISTOPHER,
  Anne 22
  Frances 22
  Mary 83
CINNE,
  Elizabeth 64
CLARK,
  Anne 55
  Berkley 2
  Bersheby 2
  Chloe 41
  Frances 8
  Jemima 14
  Lucretia 21
  Lucy 37
  Mary 7, 8, 48
  Mary Ann 99
  Nancy 37
CLATTERBACK - CLATTERBUCK,
  Elizabeth 33
  Judith 96
  Molly 42
  Sarah 6
  Sharlotte 69
  Susanna 74
CLIFTON,
  Elizabeth 97
CLINCH,
  Rachel 70
CLORE,
  Anna 97
  Frances 95
  Rosany 73
COCKE,
  Frances 85
  Sarah 55
COCKRINE - COCHRAN,
  Eleanor 37

COFFER,
  Rhode 41
COFFMAN,
  Lydia 88
COGHILL,
  Ann 33
  Catherine 46
  Susanna 70
COLE,
  Elizabeth 84
COLEMAN,
  Elizabeth 96
  Mary 79
  Nancy 16
  Polly 77
  Sally 77, 78
COLLENCE,
  Margaret 29
COLLINS,
  Franky 92
  Jane 87
  Nancy 42
  Nanny 34
  Peggy 11
  Penelope 11
  Susanna 25
COLLEY - COLLY,
  Ann 59, 60
COLVERT,
  Nancy 23
COLVIN,
  Elizabeth 23
  Lucy 14
  Mary 82
  Nancy 17
  Priscilla 49
  Susanna 91
COMPTON,
  Elizabeth 72, 74
CONDY,
  Sally 90
CONNER,
  Elizabeth 17
  Milly 92
  Sally M. 92
COOK,
  Anne 4, 92
  Elizabeth 98
COONS,
  Anna 18
  Ann 25
  Caty 97
  Elizabeth 73
  Mary 101
COOPER,
  Susanna 96
CORBIN,
  Ann 25
  Elizabeth 46, 61
  Ellen 69
  Esther 31
  Frency (?) 99
  Lucy 53
  Susanna 24
CORLEY,
  Mary 91
CORNELIUS,
  Hannah 86
  Rebecca 87
CORNETT,
  Matilda 62
COSPER,
  Ann 81
  Betsy 82
  Catherine 82
COVINGTON,
  Gillean 13
  Lucy 30
  Peggy 11
COWGILL,
  Sarah 85
COWIN,
  Mary 63

COWNE,
 Elizabeth 17
 Esther 53
COX,
 Mary 60
CRAIN,
 Nancy 76
 Polly 79
CRAWFORD,
 Elizabeth 70
 Mary 27
CRAWLEY,
 Elizabeth 91
CREAL - CREEL,
 Nancy 3, 85
 Polly 77
CRIGLER,
 Anna 49
 Sally 54
CRISAL,
 Mary 13
CRITTENDEN,
 Lucy 95
CROW,
 Ellender 68
CRUTHER,
 Elizabeth 83
 Sally 35
CULLEN,
 Dorcas 3
CUMMINS,
 Abigail 78
CUNNINGHAM,
 Nancy 27
 Sarah 22
CURTIS,
 Elizabeth 40
 Fanny 4
 Nancy 68

DAHE,
 Rachel 65
DAKE,
 Charity 45
DANIEL,
 Calay 10
 Celey 10
DARNOLD,
 Mary 60
DAVIS,
 Mary 41, 67
DAWLING,
 Nancy 33
DAYLAND,
 Margaret 60
DEALE,
 Rosanna 48
DEBOURD,
 Margaret 24
DELANIE - DULANEY,
 Delilah 50
 Hannah 32
 Jeannetta 14, 15
 Joanna 58
 Milly 31
DENANY,
 Frances 36
DENNIS,
 Sarah 44
DICKEN,
 Ann 100
 Frances 8
 Mary 98
DILL,
 Mary 78
DILLARD,
 Betsey 3
DILLIN,
 Ann 3
DOBBS - DOBS,
 Mary 61
DODSON,
 Anna 10

DODSON (Continued),
 Lucy 52
 Nelly 72
 Peggy 6
DOGAN,
 Jane 98
DOGGETT,
 Betty 9
 Elizabeth 42
 Judy 54
 Sally 24
 Susanna 71
DONAWAY - DUNAWAY,
 Mary 77
DOUGLAS,
 Histher 65
DUFF,
 Nancy 42
DUKE,
 Elener 24
 Rachel 65
DULANEY,
 Elizabeth L. 32
 Harriet 30
 Susanna 12
DUNCAN,
 Elizabeth 76
 Liney 53
 Lucy 89
 Mary 86
 Tressy 37
DUNNAWAY,
 Lucy 40
DUVAL,
 Ellis 28
 Lucy 57
 Susanna 73
DYKE,
 Anne 39
 Esther 66
 Rebecca 54

EARLY,
 Mary 66
EARROL,
 Susanna 65
EASTHAM,
 Betty 4
 Eliza 55
EDDINS,
 Elizabeth 39
EDGE,
 Lydia 35
EDMONDS,
 Ann 7
EDRINGTON,
 Elizabeth 65
 Jane 29
EDWARDS,
 Lucy 9
 Mary 15
 Polly 91
ELDRIDGE,
 Martha 58
EMBRY,
 Elizabeth 67
 Sally 67
ESTES,
 Frances 40
 Nancy 9, 70
 Polly 9, 34
ETHENTON - ETHINGTON,
 Agatha 95
 Sally 98
ETHERTON,
 Fanny 31
 Lucy 98
EVANS,
 Sally 45

FARLER - FARLEY,
 Becca (2) 10

FARMER,
 Elizabeth 95
 Jane 69
 Polly 13
FARROW,
 Elizabeth 79
 Polly 31
FAVER - FAVOR,
 Ann 68
 Frances 51
 Rosamond 51
FAULCONER,
 Mary 59
 Patsey 72
 Ursula 56
FAYE,
 Elizabeth 82
FEAGINS,
 Nancy 38
FENNEL - FENNELL,
 Frances 1, 45
 Hannah 56
 Lucy 33
 Mary Ann 66
FERGUSON,
 Elizabeth 58
 Lucy 77
 Polly O. 47
FEWEL - FEWELL,
 Elizabeth 102
 Fanny 86
 Sarah 74
FICKLIN,
 Harriet 81
FIDDLE,
 Sarah 33
FIELD,
 Jane 55
FINCHAM,
 Elizabeth 80
 Polly 29
 Sarah 82
 Susanna (2) 20
FINKS,
 Elizabeth 35
 Lucy 92
 Nancy 82
FINNELL,
 Alice 101
FISHBACK,
 Sally 87
 Sarah 9
FLESHMAN,
 Elizabeth 77
 Rachel 41
FLETCHER,
 Jane 67
FLORENCE,
 Mary 54
FLOYD,
 Mary 48
 Susanna 47
FOGG,
 Henrietta 87
FORE,
 Polly 69
FOSTER,
 Elizabeth 34
 Nancy 35
 Rebecca 88
FOUSHEE,
 Ann 8
 Elizabeth 28
 Susanna 33
FRANKLIN,
 Frankey 40
FRAZIER,
 Nancy 99
FREEMAN,
 Elizabeth 23, 53
 Priscilla 42
 Sarah 53

FRISTOE,
  Nancy 8
FRY,
  Nancy 9
FRYER,
  Nancy 36
  Rachel 87
  Stalley 69
FURGESON,
  Patsy 89

GAINES,
  Ann (2) 8
  Ann G. 38
  Catharine A. 58
  Caty 76
  Clarissa A. 101
  Dolly 43
  Elizabeth 4, 22, 88
  Esther 4
  Hannah 27
  Isabella 101
  Lucretia 14
  Lucy 26
  Malinda 57
  Mary 68, 77
  Nancy 20
  Peggy 74
  Polly 7, 8, 68
  Roda 33
  Sally 76
  Susan W. 27
  Susanna 1
GARNER,
  Catherine 71
  Delphia 91
  Elizabeth 89
GARNETT,
  Anna 98
  Avee 69
  Caty 63
  Dorothea 45
  Elizabeth 37, 58
  Fanny 74
  Jallah 74
  Lucy 64
  Mary 93
  Nancy 54
  Patsey 62
  Polly 48
GARRETT - GARROTT,
  Dorothy 45
  Polly 59
  Rachel 59
GARWOOD,
  Esther 50
  Susanna 46
GAUNT,
  Agatha 62
  Elizabeth 40
  Sally 94
GEORGE,
  Susanna 19
GIBBS,
  Milly 21
  Polly Ester 3
GIBSON,
  Abby 47
  Nancy 9
GIN,
  Mary 99
GLASS,
  Lavinia 53
  Sarah 65
GOLDEN,
  Celia 72
  Nancy 75
GOOD,
  Susanna 87
GOODMAN,
  Elizabeth (2) 30
  Usley 91

GOOGE,
  Lucy 39
  Sally 25
  Susanna 19
GORE,
  Caty 84
  Elizabeth 11
  Janny 93
  Peggy 55
GOSNEY,
  Fanny 95
  Lucy 28
  Molly 63
GRADY,
  Eleanor 39
GRANT,
  Jemima 32
GRAVES,
  Elizabeth 96
  Nancy 50
  Nancy Nelson 57
  Sarah 37
  Susanna 36
GRAY,
  Dolly 57
  Polly 71
  Rebecca 6
GREEN,
  Anne 33
  Betsey 26
  Elizabeth (2) 15, 57, 72
  Frances 17
  Joyce 3
  Margaret 19
  Mary B. 81
  May 93
  Milly 86
  Polly 90
GREENWAY,
  Elizabeth Ann 42
  Mary 83
GREGORY,
  Barbara 52
GRIFFIN,
  Frances H. 12
  Mary 12
GRIGSBY,
  Mildred 53
  Susanna 96
GRIMSLEY,
  Janny 15
  Nancy 70
GRINNAN,
  Ann 75
GROVES,
  Mary 65
GUINN,
  Frances 93
  Hepsaba 27
  Polly 64
GULLY,
  Mary 64

HADDOX,
  Janny 27
HADEN,
  Susanna 83
HAINES - HAINS,
  Abigail 92
  Hester 67
HALE,
  Joanna 88
HALL,
  Elizabeth 36, 77
  Nancy 11
HALOR,
  Clara 11
HAM --,
  Frances 27
HANBACK,
  Susanna 84
HAND,
  Polly 34

HANES,
  Amelia 77
HANEY - HANYE,
  Elizabeth 66
  Mary 42
HANSBROUGH,
  Patsey 69
HANSON,
  Catherine 64
HARDEN,
  Elizabeth 58
  Frances 7, 14
  Sarah 29, 84
HARFORD,
  Alice 96
HARLAN,
  Nancy 20
HARPER,
  Elizabeth 24
  Martha 14
  Sally 81
HARRIS,
  Elizabeth 5
  Mary 5
  Sarah 47
HARRISON,
  Ann 80
  Nelly 47
HARSBARGER,
  Elizabeth 70
HARVEY,
  Catherine 87
  Margaret 31
  Nancy 21
HASBY,
  Lydia 98
HAWKINS,
  Agnes 96
  Ann 83
  Azubah 59
  Betsy 71
  Betty 71
  Elizabeth 23
  Mary 40
  Nancy 18
  Sally 89
  Sarah 5, 56
HAY,
  Anna 24
HAYNES,
  Lydia 37
  Mary 93
HAYNIE,
  Elizabeth 40
HAYWOOD,
  Debby 35
  Elizabeth 93
  Martha 56
  Mary Ann 26
HEATON,
  Abigail 83
  Elizabeth 1
  Hannah 44
  Ruth 92
HENDERSON,
  Winney 92
HENDRICK,
  Elizabeth 28
  Milly 93
HENSLEY,
  Nancy 51
  Susanna 68
HERIN,
  Polly 31
HERNDON,
  Martha W. 14
  Rachel 96
HERRIN,
  Elizabeth 64
HERVEY,
  Margaret 31
HETON,
  Sarah (2) 44

HIGGINSTON,
  Betsey 35
HILL,
  Agnes 82
  Ann 74
  Elizabeth 93
  Fanny 40
  Frances 69
  Lucy 66
  Lydia 17
  Nancy 58
  Patsey 23
  Polly 4, 23
  Sarah 12
  Susanna 55
HILTON,
  Elizabeth 29
  Mary 10
HISLE,
  Betsy 22
  Fanny 58
  Lucy 29
  Mary 54
  Polly 46
  Sally 99
  Susanna 99
HOLLAND,
  Damsel 55
  Elizabeth 18
HOLLOWAY - HOLOWAY,
  Abigail 85
  Jemima 52
  Mary 6
HOLMES - HOMES,
  Nancy 74
  Polly 99
HOPKINS,
  Anne 43
  Fanny 62
  Jane 30
HOPPER,
  Frances 7
  Martha 14
  Nancy 91
HORNER,
  Maria 10
HORSLEY,
  Nancy 42
HORTON,
  Milly 20
  Nancy 20
HOUGHTON,
  Sarah 50
HOUSE,
  Mary 34
HOUTON,
  Anne (2) 1
HOWE,
  Betsy R. 24
HUANS,
  Polly 26
HUDNELL,
  Jemimah 99
HUDSON,
  Betsy 100
  Caty 37
  Nancy 14
  Polly 9
HUFFMAN - HUFMAN,
  Caty 49
  Elizabeth 36, (2) 48,102
  Eve 49
  Hannah 34, 70
  Mary 17, 35, 61, 85
  Susanna 18
HUGHES,
  Elizabeth 4, 36
  Lucy 12, 36, 94
  Mary 88
  Nancy 35, 62, 88
  Peggy 101
  Polly 64

HUME,
  Anne 18, 97
  Frances 92
  Sally 27
  Sarah 41
HUMPHREY,
  Charity 10
HUNT,
  Elizabeth 22
  Fanny 52
  Mary 1
HURT,
  Elizabeth 22
  Frankey 9
  Hannah 46
HUSE,
  Elizabeth 63

INSKEEP,
  Sarah 37
  Susanna 7

JACKSON,
  Elizabeth 81
  Sarah 43
JAMES,
  Elizabeth 6
JARRELL,
  Eleanor 60
  Elizaan 51
  Mary 42
JASPER,
  Ramey 46
JEFFRIES,
  ELizabeth 101
  Sarah 70
JENKINS,
  Agatha 51
  Amelia 31
  Anne 20
  Celia 56
  Clara 58, 73
  Delilah 51
  Ellen 52
  Frances 94
  Julia 21
  Lucy 63
  Lydia 46
  Mary 20
  Milley 52
  Nancy 19, 57, 67
  Patsey 80
  Peggy 52
  Phoebe 66
  Polly 74
  Rebecca 52
  Sarah (2) 51
JENNETT,
  Jemima 7
JENNINGS,
  Elizabeth 25
  Lucy 31
  Nancy 73
  Sarah 68
JETT,
  Alice 67
  Anne 63
  Isabella 79
  Lavinia 40
  Sally 12
  Sarah 46
  Susanna (2) 56
JEWS,
  Nancy 25
JOHNSON - JOHNSTON,
  Ames (2) 26
  Dinah 10
  Elizabeth 25, 31
  Lucy 85
  Mary Ann 26
  Milly 72
  Nancy 60

JOHNSON - JOHNSTON, (Continued),
  Sarah 13, 29
  Sinah 13
JOLLETT,
  Susannah (2) 10
JOLLY,
  Frances 36
JONES,
  Anna 50
  Catherine 3
  Elizabeth 5, 39, 46, 50
  Frances 18
  Joannah 21
  Lucinda 52
  Lucy 74
  Molly 37
  Nancy 43
  Polly 47
  Sarah 14, 43
  Susanna 40
JORDAN,
  Rachel 78

KABLER,
  Anna 100
  Nancy 7
KANSLAR,
  Elizabeth 19
KEARN,
  Mary N. 25
KEBBEN,
  Polly 33
KEGG,
  Thirza 51
KELLY,
  Ann 89
  Nancy 9
  Polly 43
  Susanna 85
KENNADY,
  Molly 91
KENNARD,
  Lotty 14
  Milley 54
KEY,
  Thiza 51
KILBY,
  Fanny 26
  Polly 43
KING,
  Anne 60
  Charlotte 2
KINNARD,
  Elizabeth 37
  Milly 30
  Sally 65
KIRTLY,
  Nancy 66
  Sarah 67, 75
KLINE,
  Peggy, 91

LAMPKIN,
  Anne 70
  Betsy 85
  Sally 55
LANDRUM,
  Elizabeth 29
LANE,
  Polly 57
LATHAM,
  Elizabeth 66
  Lucy 32
  Mary 73
LAWAN,
  Peggy 49
LAWLER,
  Polly 49
  Susanna 50
LEAR,
  Jemima (2) 17

LEATHERER,
Charlotte 8
LEATHERS,
Patsey 30
Phoebe 34
LEAVELL,
Elizabeth F. 34
Sarah 13, 28
LEWIS,
Frances 42
Jemima 91
Nancy 20
Sarah 56
Susanna 95
LIGHTFOOT,
Ann 37
Martha (2) 31
LILLARD,
Elizabeth 101
Frances 79
Nancy 14
Patsey 74
Polly 9, 19
LINDSEY,
Margaret 10
LIPP,
Elizabeth 39
LITTLE,
Mary 65
Nancy 2
LLOYD,
Fannie (2) 11
LONG,
Frances 62
Lucy 65
Mary 2, 61
Milly 44
Nancy 11
Sarah 11
LOURY,
Elizabeth 82
LOVELL,
Elizabeth 87
Frances 97
LUCAS,
Elizabeth 84
Jemima 97
Polly 87
LUCKIE,
Alice 87

MADDOX,
Elizabeth 75
Mary 28
MAGRUDER,
Ruth 5
MAJOR,
Elizabeth 56
Frankey 73
Mary 68
MANSFIELD,
Frankey 1
MANUEL,
Keziah 44
MARDES,
Nancy 72
MARRIFIELD,
Frances 1
MARSHALL,
Becky 45
Betsy 70
Elizabeth 4
Gilly 54
Hannah 91
Lucy 87
Peggy 10, 79
Polly 99
Rhoda 45
Sally 65, 75
MARSTON,
Polly 80
MARYE,
Mildred G. 38
MASON,
Betsy 47

MASON (Continued),
Elizabeth 48
Frances 90
Judith 25
Lucy 99
Mary 39
Nancy 84
Polly 47
Sarah 38
MATTHEWS - MATHEWS,
Catherine 16
Mary Ann 24
Sarah 5
MAUCK,
Elizabeth 38
MAURY,
Polly 90
MAYER,
Sally 101
MAYLAND,
Anna Mag 19
MC ALISTER - MC ALLISTER,
Betty 33
Elizabeth 80
MC CALLASTER,
Elizabeth 80
MC CARTY,
Polly 74
MC CAULEY,
Polly 71
MC CLANAHAN,
Lucy 13
Molly 90
MC DOGLE,
Elizabeth 30
MC DONALD,
Elenor 32
MC DUGLEY,
Sarah 60
MC GANNON,
Alice 16
MC GRUDER,
Ruthy 5
MC GUINN,
Nancy 70
Winny 1
MC KELBIN,
Margaret 31
MC KENSEY,
Anne 52
Polly 68
MC QUEEN,
Fanny 30
Nancy 79
Polly 7
Winny 1
MC QUIN,
Nancy 70
MEADE,
Polly 15
MEDLEY,
Milly 86
MENEFEE,
Ann S. 2
Cassandra 12
Elizabeth 20
Frances 68
Hannah 25
Jane 88
Milly 92, 100
Polly 67, 78
Tabitha 13
MERRY,
Elizabeth 39
MILLER,
Aggy 86
Anna 6
Elizabeth 78
Polly 15, 53
Sally 66
Sophia 75
MILLS,
Susanna 22

MITCHELL,
Nancy 58
Peggy 36, 76
Sarah 64, 93
MONROE,
Judith 18
Maria 67
Mary 75
Sally 25
MOORE,
Abigail 61
Ann 60
Anna 13
Elizabeth 46, 77
Palema 61
Polly 84
MORGAN,
Caty 94
Lucy (2) 33
MORRIS,
Dolly 98
Elizabeth 7, 15, 20
Esther 63
Kelly 12
Polly 20, 23, 84
MORTON,
Ellen 71
MOSS,
Betsey 68
Mary 73
MOZINGO,
Ann 38
Frances 4
Mary 98
MURPHY - MURFEY,
Anna 71
Elizabeth 60, 78
Rebecca 23
MYRTLE,
Anne 45
Isabel 64
Lucy 68

NALLE,
Amy 41
Clary 40
Nancy 24
NEALS,
Susanna 15
NEATHERS,
Nancy 44
NEWBY,
Peggy 78
NEWTON,
Cynthia 48
Elizabeth 79
Jannet 64
Mary 62
NICHOLSON,
Jane 44
Nelly 61
NORMAN,
Agge 40
Elizabeth 38
Frances 21
Jemima 58
Keziah 56
Nancy 7
Nancy (Jennings) 16
Polly 12, 84
NOWLIN,
Caty 52
NOWMAN,
Rosy 35

ODER - ODOR,
Ann 90
Elizabeth 41
Margaret 35
Nancy 15
Sally 28
OLIVE,
Esther 16

OLIVER,
  Sally 17, 44
ONEALS,
  Jane 76

PAINE,
  Frances 48
PALMER,
  Nancy 45
PARKS,
  Peggy 66
  Sally 92
PARSONS,
  Polly 96
PARTLOW,
  Catherine 63
  Lucy 63
  Patsey 6, 10
  Polly 9
  Sally Reynolds 65
PASSONS,
  Fanny 94
  Isabell 45
PATON - PATTON,
  Alice 3
  Hannah 31
PAUL,
  Elizabeth 1
PAYNE,
  Frances 72
PAYTON,
  Margaret 96
  Winney 32
PEMBLETON,
  Elizabeth 41
PENDLETON,
  Elizabeth 69
  Frances 13
  Joanna 82
  Sally 86
PENNELL,
  Nancy 78
PETTINGER,
  Rebecca 28
PETTY,
  Dolly 54
  Elizabeth 35
  Nancy 6
  Susanna 77
PEYTON,
  Margaret 96
  Mary 32
  Phebe 32
PHILLIPS,
  Mary 19
PICKETT,
  Nancy 78
PIERCE,
  Elizabeth (2) 27, 84
  Fanny 18
  Nancy (2) 17
  Rosannah 46
  Sallie 19
PINER,
  Ann 89
  Susanna 2
PINKARD,
  Polly 76
PINNELL,
  Lucy 94
  Patty 42
PLUNCKETT,
  Betsy 26
POLLARD,
  Amelia 9
  Ann C. 51
POPHAM,
  Rachel Evins 77
PORTER,
  Anna 65
  Betsey 61
  Fanny 5

PORTER, (Continued),
  Nancy 82
  Sally 34
POULTER,
  Eleanor 79
  Elizabeth 56
POUND,
  Molly 81
POWELL,
  Ann 21, 87
  Elizabeth 49
  Martha 22
  Mary 76
  Tomsey 21
  Towsey 21
PRATT,
  Jane 97
PRICE,
  Nancy 97
PRIEST,
  Mary 2
  Elizabeth 9
PROVINCE,
  Esther 79
PULLIAM,
  Agnes 54
  Elizabeth 93
  Frances (2) 50
  Mary 28
  Nancy 96
  Winny 92
PULMAN,
  Anna 42
PUP,
  Sally 3
PUSEY - PUSY,
  Rachel 50
PUTMAN,
  Betty 49
  Frances 60

QUINN,
  Frances 93
  Sally 94

RAINES,
  Delphia 21
  Elizabeth 82
  Mildred 88
RAKESTRAW,
  Birley 74
RAMBOTTOM,
  Hannah 28
RAMEY,
  Caty 12
  Fanny 62
RANDOLPH,
  Frances 66
  Mahala 43
RATLIFF,
  Sarah 36
REA,
  Lucy 16
READ,
  Lucy 16, 48
REASONS,
  Milly 6
REDMAN,
  Milly 73
REECE,
  Agnes 14
REED,
  Susanna 53
  Tabitha 20
REINS,
  Elizabeth 57
REMINE,
  Mary 51
RESOR,
  Catherine 86
RETHERFORD,
  Abigail 6

REVERCOMB,
  Elizabeth 85
REYNOLDS,
  Jane 77
RICE,
  Ann 102
RICH,
  Effie 56
RICHARDS,
  Elizabeth 50
  Roda 47
RICHERSON - RICHARDSON,
  Elizabeth 2
  Nancy 21
RIDER,
  Mary 64
ROACH,
  Lettice 59
ROBBINS,
  Nancy 52
ROBERTS,
  Betsey 75
  Elizabeth 43
  Ginnet 5
  Jemima 58
  Polly 23
  Sarah 36, 85
  Tary 82
RODLHEIFER,
  Sarah 100
ROEBUCK,
  Elizabeth 44
  Judith 19
ROGERS,
  Elizabeth 81
  Frances 90
  Margaret 101
ROSS,
  Frances 88
  Nelly 22
ROSSON - ROSSEN,
  Frances 84
  Margaret 27
  Sukey 67
ROUTT,
  Ann 28
  Elizabeth 96
  Peggy 13
ROWE,
  Anne 36
  Fanny 39
ROYSTER,
  Matilda C. 92
RUCKER,
  Frankey 1
  Nancy 44
RUSH,
  Sally 37, 82

SAMPSON,
  Rhoda 4
  Sally 85
SAMUEL,
  Fanny 45
  Polly 70
SANFORD,
  Julia 47
  Lucy 62
SANDERS,
  Betsy 70
  Elizabeth 80
  Mary 79
SCOTT,
  Jany 40
  Jenny 81
  Jerusha 81
  Nancy 25
  Phoebe 68
  Polly 64
  Sarah 18
SEBREE,
  Fanny 94

SEDWICK,
  Sally 65
SETTLE,
  Elizabeth 97
  Jane 40
  Linney 20
  Lucy 3
  Polly 39
  Tabitha 15
  Tryphine 57
SEWRIGHT,
  Elizabeth 13
SHACKELFORD - SHACKLEFORD,
  Elizabeth 66
  Frances 54
  Lucy 22
  Maria 41
  Milly 38
  Nancy 86
  Susanna 17
  Winny 90
SHANNON,
  Eliza 2
SHARP - SHARPE,
  Elizabeth 3
  Esther 2
SHAVER,
  Polly 31
SHAW,
  Nancy 85
SHELTON,
  Lucy 98
SHEPHERD,
  Mary 23
SHERWOOD,
  Mary 86
SHINGLETON,
  Sally (2) 89
SHIP - SHIPP,
  Lucy 102
  Nancy 59
SHIRER,
  Sarah 21
SHORT,
  Sarah 21
SHOTWELL,
  Elizabeth 83
SIMMS - SIMS,
  Avie 23
  Betsey 72
  Elizabeth T. 32
  Mary (2) 39, 69
  Nancy 91
  Sally 50
  Sarah 15, 51, 73
SINE,
  Phebe 80
SISK,
  Lavinia 29
  Milly 51
  Susan 95
SISSON,
  Elizabeth 34
SLAUGHTER,
  Anne 55
  Elizabeth 28, 35
  Lucinda 59
  Mildred 31
SLEET,
  Ursie 61
SMEDE,
  Elizabeth 38
SMITH,
  Amy 3
  Anne 28, 43, 76, 100
  Anne Bohannon 43
  Betsy 62
  Catherine 5
  Clara 101
  Clarissa B. 90
  Elizabeth (2) 43, 46, 52,
                72

SMITH (CONTINUED),
  Laura 25
  Leah 19
  Mary 12, 75
  Patty 80
  Polly 75
  Sally 23
  Sarah 19
  Susanna 33, 82, 84
SMOOTE,
  Sally 18
SNYDER,
  Judy 57
  Susanna 73
SOUTHER,
  Elizabeth 21
SPENCER,
  Catherine 99
  Charity 22
  Elizabeth 41
  Rachel 61
SPILLER,
  Lucy 57
  Susanna 22
SPILMAN,
  Elizabeth 78
  Susanna 28
SPOTSWOOD,
  Mary 93
STALLARD,
  - - 75
  Susanna 30
STANTON,
  Mary 14, 58
STAPLEMAN,
  Eleanor 4
STEPTOE,
  Jamijah 99
STEWARD,
  Sally 62
STIPE,
  Elizabeth 24
STOKES,
  Ann 7
STOKESBURY,
  Elizabeth 26
  Susanna 57
STOMSIFER,
  Mary 48
STONE,
  Nancy 13
STORY,
  Anne 100
  Elizabeth 52
  Jenny 97
STOUT,
  Anne 93
  Lydia 39
STROTHER,
  Behethelen 47
  Elizabeth 49, 89
  Gilly C. 32
  Lucy 2
  Mary 63
  Mildred 14
  Polly 16, 95
  Sally 47
  Sarah 69
STURMAN,
  Susanna 68
SUDDETH - SUDDITH,
  Leanah 17
  Sally 79
SULLIVAN,
  Nancy 84
SUTHERLAND,
  Jemimah 60
  Nancy 98
SUTTLE,
  Juda 68
SUTTON,
  Lucy 2

SUTTON (Continued),
  Nancy 45
SWINDLER,
  Anne 4
  Chloe 17
  Elizabeth 71
  Henrietta 69
  Susanna 22

TALIAFERRO,
  Alice 88, 89
  Kitty 8
  Mary 74
  Sally 58
TANNEHILL,
  Keziah 19
TAPP,
  Ann (2) 2
  Anna 25
  Nancy 57
  Sally 78
  Susanna 19, 62
TATUM,
  Sarah 80
TAYLOR,
  Alice 84
  Anne Read 61
TERRELL - TERRILL,
  Mary 76
  Nancy 35
  Sally 75
TERRY,
  Mary 41
  Nancy 56
THOMAS,
  Caty 5
  Rhoda 4
  Sarah 65
THOMPSON,
  Frances 3
  Isabella 12
THORNHILL,
  Elizabeth 46
  Lucy 71
THORNTON,
  Frances 42, 43
  Lucy 94
THRELKELD,
  Anne 16
  Elizabeth 21, 100
  Margaret 10
  Mary 38, 57
  Nancy 72
  Nelly 95
  Polly 27
  Rachel 91
  Ruth 26
  Susanna 28
THUD,
  Ann 3
TINSLEY,
  Elizabeth 74
  Mildred 76
  Milly 35
TOBIN,
  Nancy 90
  Peggy 93
  Rebecca 79
TOMLIN,
  Mary 73
THOMPKINS,
  Rachel 7
TOWLES,
  Frances 98
  Jane 80
  Lucy 97
  Mary 84
  Sally 76
TRENTON,
  Betsey 81
TRIMBLE,
  Lydia 3

TRIPLETT,
  Nancy 25
  Polly 65
  Sally H. 27
TUCKER,
  JEMIMAH 66
  Lavinia 79
  Uphias 90
TURNER,
  Betsey 91
  Dicy 22
  Mary 75
  Nancy 18, 54, 60
  Polly 22
  Sally 78
  Susanna 37
TURNHAM,
  Elizabeth 86
TUTT,
  Amelia 71
  Ann 64
  Nancy 87
  Polly 45
  Sarah 76
TWENTIMAN,
  Betsy 38
  Lucy 5
  Polly 9
TWYMAN,
  Ann 92
  Frances 26

UNDERWOOD,
  Annie 2
  Mary 55
  Nancy 2
UTTERBACK,
  Crissey 99
  Mag 26
  Mary 75
  Priscilla 71
  Sally 67
  Sarah 5
  Susanna 68
UTZ,
  Elizabeth 87
  Rachel 95

VAN DIKE,
  Mary 85
VASS,
  Catherine 5
VAUGHAN,
  Betsey 92
  Eleanor (2) 7
  Elizabeth 76
  Fanny 69
  Harriet Byron 25
  Lucy 68
  Mary 76
  Nancy 24
VAWTER,
  Alpha 79
VERNON,
  Sarah 95
  Sucky 94
VINCE,
  Mary 45
VINT,
  Catherine 69
VISECARVER,
  Mary 28
VOSS,
  Catherine 5
  Harriet 61

WAGGONER - WAGONER,
  Ann 49
  Betsey 59
  Fanny 55
  Lucy 96
  Mary 53

WAGGONER - WAGONER,
  Polly 63
  Sarah 55
WALDEN,
  Polly 1
WALKER,
  Mary 23
  Mildred 21, 94
  Nancy 53
  Sarah 64
WALLACE - WALLIS,
  Malinda 61
  Matilda 61
  Susanna 74
WALL - WALLE,
  Anne 28
  Elizabeth 8
  Lucy 27
  Mary 34, 94
  Nancy 33
WARD,
  Anne 24, 95
  Elizabeth 69
  Judith 8
  Maria 29
  Mary 48
  Peggy 6
  Sally 29
WARNER,
  Mary 56
WARREN,
  Elizabeth 36
WASHINGTON,
  Ann 69
WATERSPON,
  Winifred 20, 78
WATTS,
  Agatha 91
  Catherine 15
  Elizabeth 93
  Sally 67, 83
WAUGH,
  Mary L. 88
WAYLAND,
  Anne 100
  Eleanor 95
WEAKLY - WEAKLEY - WEEKLY,
  Betsy 52
  Jemimah 6
  Nancy 51, 52
  Susanna 51
WEATHERALL,
  Elener 12
WEAVER,
  Dinah 36
  Elizabeth 20, 97
  Frances 14
  Hannah 8
  Mary 5
  Nancy 14
WEST,
  Ann 87
  Rebecca 78
WESTALL,
  Sally 89
WHARTON,
  Polly 59
  Sally 60
WHEATLY,
  Mary 15
  Sally 7
WHITE,
  Eliza C. 1
  Elizabeth 4
  Margaret 47
  Peggy 1
  Rachel 81
  Susanna 11, 98
WHITEHEAD,
  Sarah 89
WHITELEY,
  Elizabeth 61

WHITLEDGE,
  Jane 13
WICOFF,
  Susanna 83
WIGGINTON,
  Nancy 24
WILEY,
  Elizabeth 57
  Lydia 33
  Mary 59
WILHOIT,
  Elizabeth 62
  Fanny 60
  Frances 60
  Julia 85
  Margaret 100
  Mary 72
  Nancy 43
  Polly 63, 80
WILKERSON,
  Lucy 17
WILLEY,
  Jane 41
WILLIAMS,
  Dorcas 41
  Elizabeth 20
  Ellen 73
  Mary 101
  Mary Ann 11
  Sally 77
  Sarah 43, 46
WILLIS,
  Arcy 98
  Jane 46, 71
WILLSON - WILSON,
  Caty (2) 55
  Elizabeth 8
WINSTON,
  Sally 32
WISE,
  Nancy 60
  Peggy 36
WITHERALL,
  Polly 90
WITHERS,
  Nancy 40
WOOD,
  Ann 62
  Betsy 32
  Dinah 7
  Elizabeth 53
WOODARD,
  Hannah 64
  Margaret 29
  Mary 35
WOODWARD,
  Ann 18
  Nancy 18, 46
WORTHAM,
  Charlotte 23
WRIGHT,
  Alice 63
  Frances 55
  Hannah 94
  Lucy 83, 90
  Margaret 10
  Sarah 90

YAGER,
  Dinah 83
  Elizabeth 100
  Fanny 47
  Hannah 100
  Jemima 94, 100
  Mary 24
  Rosanna 82
YANCY,
  Eleanor 44
  Frances 26, 32
  Lucy 63
  Malinda 16
  Mary Ann 53

YANCY (Continued),
  Philadelphia 62
  Polly 63
YATES,
  Barbara 55
  Betsey 23
  Eliza 94
  Elizabeth 10, 24
  Frances 41, 101
  Lucy 61
  Milly 8
  Nancy 54, 67
  Patsey 53
  Polly 13, 56
  Sally 11, 32
YEAGER,
  Patty 23
YOUNG,
  Amey 76
  Anne 99
YOWELL,
  Elizabeth 85
  Nancy 36
  Sarah 5
  Sealy 42
  Synthia 18

ZIGLER,
  Elizabeth 102
  Leanna 88
ZIMMERMAN,
  Eleanor 20
  Lucy 33
  Margaret 59
  Mary 5
  Mildred 86
  Rosanna 77
  Suckey 11
  Susanna 47

www.ingramcontent.com/pod-product-compliance
Lightning Source LLC
Chambersburg PA
CBHW021834020426

42334CB00014B/628